Human Embryos

The Debate on Assisted Reproduction

Human Embryos

The Debate on Assisted Reproduction

C. R. AUSTIN

*Emeritus Charles Darwin Professor
of Animal Embryology, University
of Cambridge, UK*

Illustrations by
John R. Fuller

Oxford New York Tokyo
OXFORD UNIVERSITY PRESS
1989

Oxford University Press, Walton Street, Oxford OX2 6DP

Oxford New York Toronto
Delhi Bombay Calcutta Madras Karachi
Petaling Jaya Singapore Hong Kong Tokyo
Nairobi Dar es Salaam Cape Town
Melbourne Auckland

and associated companies in
Berlin Ibadan

Oxford is a trade mark of Oxford University Press

Published in the United States
by Oxford University Press, New York

British Library Cataloguing in Publication Data
Austin, C.R. (Colin Russell), 1914–
Human embryos.
1. Man. Infertility
I. Title
616.6'92
ISBN 0-19-261758-3

Library of Congress Cataloging in Publication Data
(Data available)

Set by Footnote Graphics Ltd, Warminster, Wilts
Printed in Great Britain by
The Guernsey Press Co. Ltd.
Guernsey, Channel Islands

Preface

The artificial control (or 'assistance') of human reproduction
has attracted an impressive degree of public interest in recent
years, owing chiefly to advances in technology and the conse-
quent increasing wealth of procedures that can be applied to
suppress, limit, augment, or supplant the natural reproductive
process. The elements of the technology induce a good deal
of fascination, and close attention is paid to the immediate
benefits and injuries of its application, but people feel most
deeply concerned about the control of the new technology,
and the possible consequences of its unrestricted exploitation, particularly in relation to human happiness and well-
being. It is not surprising, therefore, that vigorous debate has
been stirred, finding expression in books and articles and in
the public media, and it is wholly desirable that this should
proceed spontaneously and unfettered, as far as possible.

This book has been written with the object of assisting in
the debate, by providing information relevant to the issues
under discussion, mostly of a biological nature, and by
examining several points on which opinion is sharply
divided, in the hope that this might help in reaching acceptable compromises. The manner of treatment is intended to be
'interpretive', making technical ideas more understandable to
the non-specialist, while presenting sufficient detailed and
contemporary data to appeal to those better informed. Technical terms are defined briefly on first usage; a glossary is not
provided, but reference to the index should enable the reader
to find adequate explanation without difficulty.

Terms that need more than a mere mention at this stage are
'pre-embryo' and 'proembryo'—they are not used in this
book, although much in vogue elsewhere. The reason for
their introduction was to make it clear that the first appearance of elements that later constitute the human person is not

at the start of embryonic development, i.e. at fertilization, but some two weeks later, when the 'embryonic disc' and 'primitive streak' become recognizable; the disc and streak are destined to be 'person' while all the rest of the embryo goes to form placenta and other auxiliary structures. For the purposes of this book, it is considered more appropriate to distinguish between 'embryo' and 'fetus', despite the fact that present common usage of these terms is not helpful. The cells of the embryonic disc and primitive streak are already generally acknowledged to be the fetal primordia, so that if they, and all their successors, could be identified clearly as 'fetus', while the rest of the conceptus (by far the greater part during the first trimester of pregnancy) continued under the title 'embryo', life would be so much simpler. This point is enlarged upon in the text.

The author has tried to make the book as concise as it reasonably can be, since more detailed treatment can readily be found elsewhere—recommended comprehensive publications are references 6, 22, 52, 121, 136 and those that appear in the list of 'Further reading' at the end of the book.

The text consists first of all of a straightforward account of the anatomy and physiology of human embryonic and fetal development, with emphasis on the early stages, and an enquiry into the perennial conundrum as to when life begins. This is followed by a review of the present status of research in this field, mostly in laboratory animals but a little in human beings (into whose development research is somewhat restricted), including a brief account of genetic engineering and its potential for the diagnosis, treatment, and cure of genetic diseases, with some thought given to contentious issues such as the making of chimeras, hybrids, parthenogenones, and clones. Then we consider the reasons for infertility in men and women, and ways of overcoming it, with particular reference to the test-tube baby procedure, or IVF+ET, and its variations and alternatives, as well as associated manoeuvres such as artificial insemination-donor (formerly, but no longer 'AID') and surrogacy. In the final section, there are reflections on some ethical and legal issues currently arousing interest and debate. Attention is given also to themes on the border-line of fiction, but reflecting deeply felt anxieties often expressed by members of the public, namely, that the drive towards the treatment and cure of human reproductive and genetic problems might degenerate into a kind of ruthless eugenics, recalling Nazi dcctrine, or result in something akin to the social system described in Huxley's *Brave New World*. The text ends with a synopsis in which the main points are set out briefly. A reference list follows.

The author is indebted to the 'readers' appointed by Oxford University Press, who made a number of helpful suggestions and good points.

47 Dixon Road
Buderim
Queensland 4556
Australia
September 1988   C.R.A.

Contents

1
The natural course of events

Eggs and sperm

The development of the human embryo is normally initiated by the union of an egg and a sperm in the process of fertilization. Both egg and sperm are single cells, made up of nucleus and cytoplasm, but in structure they differ very much from each other, being highly specialized for their particular functions.

Eggs (Fig. 1.1) are unusually large cells, among the largest in the body, and each is enclosed within a thick transparent

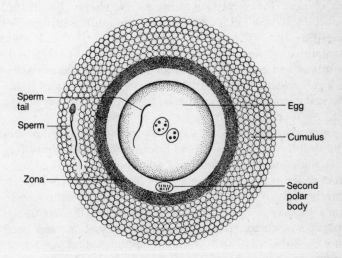

Fig. 1.1 Diagram of the human egg during fertilization, showing the zona and surrounding cumulus, through which the sperm must pass to enter the egg. The fluid-filled space between the egg and the zona contains the second polar body. Within the egg are the two pronuclei and the tail of the fertilizing sperm.

capsule, the 'zona pellucida', or zona for short. The egg cytoplasm contains, in addition to the nucleus, large numbers of different structures that represent the living machinery of the cell. Egg production takes place in the ovary, and for most of the latter part of their lives there, the eggs occupy cavities known as 'follicles', in which they are cossetted by large numbers of 'nurse' cells, constituting the 'cumulus' (Latin for cloud). When the time comes to leave the ovary, the follicle wall ruptures and the egg, accompanied by a generous layer of cumulus, is extruded ('ovulated') and seemingly picked up by the fringed ('fimbriated') end of the oviduct (Fig. 1.2). Within the oviduct, the egg awaits the attention of the sperm.

Sperm (Fig. 1.1) are small cells, about 0.05 mm long, with a compact head (mostly nucleus) and a tail. In a sense, they are stripped for action, for they lack several items common to other cells, retaining only a nucleus and some essential 'machinery' for converting nutrients into energy, but in addition they have a tail for propulsion through the surrounding medium and an 'acrosome' on the tip of the head which contains enzymes that will enable the sperm to penetrate the cumulus and zona and thus enter the egg. The sperm nucleus is a remarkably dense structure, consisting largely of tightly packed chromosomes; its shape is distinctive of every species and even subspecies.

Sperm are produced in the testis and achieve most of their ability to fertilize as they pass through the 'epididymis' (Fig. 1.3), a long tortuous tube that leads from the testis to a larger duct called the 'vas deferens'; this in turn connects with the 'urethra', the conduit through the penis. At ejaculation, secretions of accessory glands greatly augment the volume of sperm suspension passing through the system, and these contain substances that stimulate sperm swimming activity and provide the energy source on which this depends.

Both eggs and sperm carry in their nuclei the specifications for all of the characteristics of a future person, in the form of a vast number of 'genes' (from the Greek word *genos*, meaning 'descent'), packed into rod-shaped items called 'chromo-

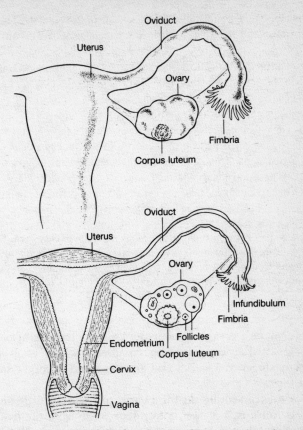

Fig. 1.2 Two aspects of the female reproductive organs, the surface view above and the sectional view below. (From ref. 1.)

somes' (from the Greek words *chroma*, meaning 'colour', and *soma*, meaning 'a body', because at certain stages they can be stained strongly with appropriate dyes). Most body cells carry the number of chromosomes typical of the human being, namely 46, but eggs and sperm when ready for fertilization have only 23 each; when they get together, the full complement is restored. The half-quota that eggs and sperm have is

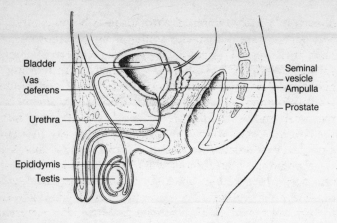

Fig. 1.3 The components of the male reproductive system. Sperm are produced in the testis and pass along the epididymis and vas deferens to enter the urethra, not far from the bladder. Important secretions are added from the ampulla, the seminal vesicles, and the prostate. (From ref. 2.)

the result of a series of events making up 'meiosis' (from the Greek word *meion*, meaning 'smaller'), which takes place in two stages referred to as the first and second 'meiotic divisions'.

For most of its life in the ovary, the egg has a distinctive round nucleus, but just before its release from the ovary at ovulation, the first meiotic division begins and the typical nucleus is replaced by a group of chromosomes (still 46 in number) which seem to have 'just appeared' (in fact, the chromosomes were there all the time but existed in a highly extended form, virtually invisible except by special microscopic techniques). In this group, the chromosomes arrange themselves in pairs, one member of each pair deriving originally from the mother of the woman whose eggs we are talking about, and the other from her father. These maternal and paternal hereditary contributions have stayed quite separate up to this point, but now a strange thing happens—parts of each in a pair of parental chromosomes become entwined and portions are exchanged, so that many chromosomes are now mixtures of genes derived from the two parental sources. What we have here is essentially a 'reshuffling' of genes and it happens in each generation, which is why inheritance in human beings, as in other mammals, is such a complex affair and never fully predictable. In the next step, half of the chromosome group is extruded from the egg in a small globule of cytoplasm known as a 'polar body'—this is the 'first' polar body, as another will be produced later, and this one does not last long, breaking up and disappearing while other events proceed. The chromosomes remaining within the egg are now only 23 in number but they also represent a *unique* collection of genes, because of the reshuffling that went on earlier. After emission of the first polar body, ovulation occurs and the egg passes into the oviduct, where the second meiotic division follows sperm penetration.

In the production of sperm—spermatogenesis—meiosis involves two successive divisions of the precursor cells, so that four functional cells are formed. The process is basically similar to meiosis in egg production, with the same kind of gene reshuffling being in evidence, but *each* of the four sperm resulting is genetically unique, and of course each has 23 chromosomes.

The congregation of eggs and sperm

When fertile intercourse takes place some 2–6 ml of semen, containing anything up to 1500 million sperm, is deposited in the vagina, and from this vast multitude much smaller numbers make their way into the uterus and then into the oviducts (Fig. 1.2). Only a small fraction of the original assembly ever reaches the upper regions of the oviducts where fertilization is to take place, the great majority falling by the wayside, so that the sperm 'reception committee' for the eggs usually amounts to only a few thousand. Even this number seems like a huge excess for the fertilization of only one or perhaps two or three eggs, but the space within the oviducts is enormous when compared to the sizes of eggs and sperm, so that a successful encounter would be rare indeed unless a large number of sperm was present.

The dramatic reduction in sperm number from vagina to site of fertilization has often prompted suggestions that there could be some kind of selection process operating. Debates on the topic have been vigorous but, as yet, convincing evidence is lacking. A basic difficulty is to explain what the selection could be *for*? Perhaps it could be the selection of sperm carrying genetic characters that would determine the *fittest* embryos. But how could sperm express selectable features underlying embryo fitness? Sperm do have surface antigens that can be detected by appropriate techniques, and the nature of these would probably be determined genetically, so it can be argued that the most immunologically acceptable sperm would be those likely to lead to the development of embryos whose surface properties were tolerable or even attractive to the female tract. Such a state of affairs is possible, and indeed there are kinds of infertility known in which the female tract is immunologically 'hostile' to the partner's sperm, and in these cases the sperm rarely, if ever, achieve fertilization. But really what many people have in mind for the 'best' sperm and the 'best' embryos are those that will lead eventually to the birth of children who will grow into the biggest, cleverest, strongest, most handsome, or most socially acceptable adults, and these ideas are well into the realms of fantasy.

Eggs arrive in the oviduct (Fig. 1.2) from the ovary at any time from the ninth to the seventeenth day after the beginning of menstruation, most often on about the fourteenth, and then for a remarkably short time (not more than about 24 hours) they retain the capacity to be fertilized and develop into normal embryos. Sperm, too, have a very brief fertile life span, which probably does not exceed 48 hours, and they may, of course, be deposited in the vagina at any stage of the menstrual cycle. That being so, the odds against fertilization would seem to be high, and indeed they are if there is only one coital event, but in fact frequent coitus is the norm. So it needs to be a damaging condition that curtails reproductive ability sufficiently for medical help to be sought, and sadly such conditions are not particularly uncommon; some, like 'pelvic inflammatory disease' are becoming more prevalent with the current trend in sexual mores, so that assistance for reproduction is increasingly in demand. The main reasons for infertility are considered in more detail in Chapter 3.

Fertilization[3,4]

Once through the cumulus and zona, the sperm attaches itself to the surface of the egg (Fig. 1.4b) and fuses with it; the sperm nucleus then passes into the egg cytoplasm and develops into the 'male pronucleus' (the term implies that there is also a female pronucleus—this develops from the egg chromosome group—and that each contains only half of the standard number of chromosomes). The act of sperm entry serves as a stimulus to the egg, which passes into a temporary resting state after the first meiotic division and seems to need this kind of 'awakening'. The response is twofold:

1. The egg chromosomes each divide in half and one group of halves is passed out of the egg in the second polar body (Fig. 1.4d). The reason for this second meiotic division in the egg is obscure; in sperm production, it helps to double the output of sperm, but there is no known use for the second polar body. The number of egg chromosomes remains unchanged by the second meiotic division (still 23) and their normal size is soon restored. However, the second polar body is proving to have special value for the diagnosis of genetic anomalies—this aspect is discussed in Chapter 2 (pp. 73–4).

2. The metabolic machinery of the egg, responsible for the living processes in the egg, are set going again (a response

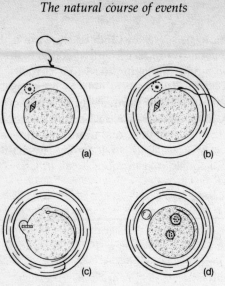

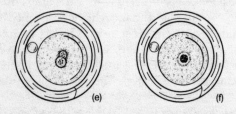

Fig. 1.4 Steps in fertilization, as seen in the rat egg. In (a), the egg chromosomes have completed the first meiotic division, and the first polar body has been produced and is seen now to be degenerating. The second meiotic division takes place (in (c)) after sperm contact with the egg (in (b)) and results in the formation of the second polar body. Entry of the sperm also causes changes in the zona (suggested by the curved lines), which make it impenetrable to all subsequent sperm. Formation and growth of pronuclei are shown in (d) and (e), and the assembly of egg and sperm chromosomes (central mass), preparatory to the first cleavage of the egg, is visible in (f).

known as 'activation') and this includes the formation and growth of the pronuclei and other events, concluding with the gathering of sperm and egg chromosomes (Fig 1.4f) about 24 hours after sperm penetration. (The details illustrated in Fig. 1.4 are based on observations on rat eggs, but the story is very similar in human eggs.)

Points of general importance are that fertilization is essential for biparental inheritance, to which the human organism appears immutably wedded (but more of this later), and that the sex of the offspring is determined at fertilization.

As mentioned above, each sperm carries 23 chromosomes, just as each egg does when ready for fertilization, and in both of these complements, one chromosome is a sex chromosome. In mammals, females are distinguished by having two X-chromosomes, while males have an X and a Y (some mammals have more complicated systems than this, but that need not trouble us here). When the gametes are formed, each egg carries an X, while the sperm have either an X or a Y. It is the sperm, therefore, that 'decides' the sex of the young person or animal. Human sperm are seemingly unique among mammals in that, if treated with the dye quinacrine, those with the Y-chromosome exhibit a small fluorescent body when examined under ultraviolet irradiation; apart from this, differences between X- and Y-bearing sperm are difficult to detect.

Clearly, it is important that only one sperm should enter the egg and take part in fertilization, and this is ensured in the great majority of cases by changes that occur both in the zona and in the surface of the egg itself—both structures become impermeable to sperm after the entry of the first, the changes constituting the 'block to polyspermy'. Neither reaction functions perfectly, however, so that polyspermy (fertilization involving two or more sperm) does occasionally take place, though probably not more than in about 2 per cent of cases under normal circumstances. The incidence is very likely to be higher when eggs are fertilized late in their fertile lives, in older women and in those under the influence of certain drugs or 'feverish' illnesses (these suggestions being based partly on observations made with laboratory animals, but supported by clinical information).[5] Polyspermy leads to 'triploidy' in the embryo, which means that it has three times the number of chromosomes as the unfertilized egg, instead of the normal twice as many, and triploid embryos develop very abnormally and usually die before birth.

Early development of the embryo[6]

With the completion of fertilization, the egg is ready for the first step in embryonic development, but at about this time, quite a different thing happens first, at least in human pregnancy—the egg releases a substance called 'early pregnancy factor (EPF)', which can be detected in the woman's blood and provides useful information should the pregnancy fail at a later stage.[7] Embryonic development then proceeds, with the egg dividing into two cells or 'blastomeres' (Gk. *blastos* bud, *meros* part) (Fig. 1.5). In the nucleus of *each* of these, there is normally a full set of 46 chromosomes, and this state of affairs is achieved by the doubling-up of chromosomes just before cell division. After a pause of about 12 hours, division of the 2-cell embryo into four cells takes place, in much the same manner as the first division; then, again, some 12 hours later, division occurs into eight cells (with, of course, chromosome duplication in each case). The process as a whole is called 'cleavage' and it is distinguished from ordinary cell division by two important features: the resulting cells are progressively smaller, and, at least until the 8-cell stage, they are structurally and functionally identical. It is quite a different matter with ordinary tissue cells—following each division and before the next one can occur, the daughter cells grow and achieve the same size and distinctive characteristics as the 'parent' cell. Up to the 8-cell stage, the cells have been held together by the zona (if the zona is removed, the cells of the embryo fall apart), but late in the 8-cell stage, or at the

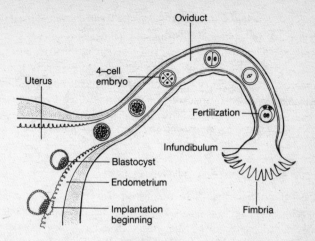

Fig. 1.5 The start and early stages of embryonic development in the human oviduct and uterus.

16-cell stage, an important new feature appears—the cells on the outside of the group become firmly attached to each other, while those inside remain unconnected. This keeps the group together and, in addition, is essential for the next change to occur—the accumulation of fluid between the cells; without the firm attachments (the 'tight junctions') between them, the fluid would escape. As the number of cells increases, through 32, 64, and so on, the volume of fluid gets bigger and the inside cells are seemingly pushed to one side; the embryo is now distinguished by the term 'blastocyst' (Gk. *blastos* bud, *kystis* bladder), and its fluid-filled cavity the 'blastocoele' (Gk. *koilos* hollow) (Figs 1.5 and 1.6). Less obvious, but demonstrable now by electron microscopy, is that the tightly connected cells on the outside have taken on a different internal structure—they have in fact begun their 'differentiation'—while the group of cells on the inside are much the same as before, though now much smaller and more numerous. The differentiation of the outside cells is most important, for its significance is that these cells now have a prescribed fate—

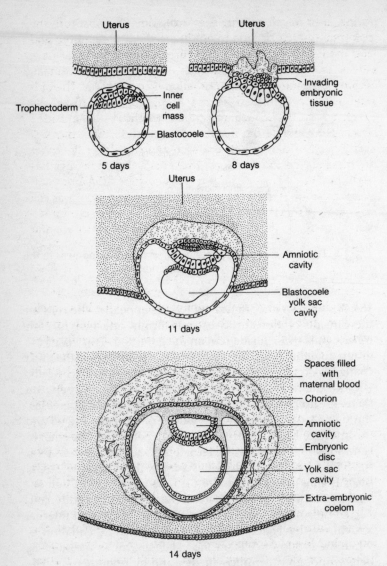

Fig. 1.6 Implantation. Diagrams are enlarged about 150 times from actual (life) size. (From ref. 8.)

during later development, they will come to constitute the 'placenta' (which attends to all the needs of the embryo and later the fetus) and related structures, and they cannot form part of the future fetus, which in due course will normally become a person. This differentiation is irreversible. The outside cells are identified as the 'trophectoderm' (from the Greek words *trophe* meaning 'nourishment', *ektos* 'outside', *derma* 'skin'), while the inside cells constitute the 'inner cell mass'. *Some* of the, as yet, undifferentiated cells of the inner cell mass are destined to form the fetus, but which ones has yet to be decided; work on the blastocysts of laboratory animals has made it clear that, though all cells of the inner cell mass are constitutionally capable of taking part in the formation of the fetus, only a few are needed for this purpose and most of them represent, instead, the forerunners of auxilliary tissues.

When the blastocyst first appears, it is still too small to be discerned by the naked eye (about 0.1 mm in diameter), but it now begins to enlarge as the amount of fluid in the blastocoele increases. Initially, the embryo was suspended freely in the oviduct secretions but it has now been moved down into the uterus. At about this time, the blastocyst releases a substance called 'platelet-activating factor', which can be detected in laboratory tests and provides a second early indication of the emerging pregnancy. When the time comes for 'implantation', the blastocyst escapes from the zona in a process picturesquely labelled 'hatching', and invades the specialized lining of the uterus (Fig. 1.6) (the 'endometrium'); this causes hormonal changes in the woman's body, notably an increase in the output of 'progesterone' by the ovary and then of 'human chorionic gonadotrophin' by the embryo itself. The rises can readily be detected by assay procedures and constitute the surest signs that a pregnancy has been initiated; the increasing level of progesterone promotes implantation by its action on the endometrium and thus favours the further development of the embryo.

As a rare event, the inner cell mass in the blastocyst may

divide into two parts, each of which can continue normal development, and this is one way in which identical twins can originate; usually, twinning occurs later, by division of a structure identified as the 'embryonic disc' or 'plate', and this will be discussed later.

Implantation and further development

Before it can implant, the blastocyst hatches and then specialized cells make their appearance on its surface, which have the ability to open a passage between the surface cells of the endometrium and burrow into the underlying tissue. In a day or two, the blastocyst disappears below the endometrial surface, with only a slight elevation to mark the point of entry. All this happens between 1 and 2 weeks after fertilization. The embryo now grows rapidly, increasing its diameter about threefold in a week, and new kinds of cells differentiate in it. At an early stage, cells on the outside multiply to form a sponge-like mass (chorion) over the embryo, and the cavities in this mass become filled with maternal blood (see Figs 1.6 and 1.7). In this way the embryo receives its nutriment and is relieved of its waste products. This does not represent a true circulation—that comes a good deal later.

By about 14 days from fertilization, the embryo has achieved a mass about ten times that of the fertilized egg, and now has two fluid-filled cavities, identified as 'amnion' and 'yolk-sac', with between them a little group of cells making up the 'embryonic disc' or 'plate' (Fig. 1.7). The cells in the central region of the disc are those that will later form the fetus, and those a little further out may also be involved in this activity, but it is difficult to say where the line should be drawn. A reasonable inference is that many of the cells of the disc are still not committed to a particular course of development, and this would be consistent with the fact that the disc has the capacity to divide into two or more parts, each of which is able to form a fetus. This is the usual stage of origin of identical twins, triplets, etc., and more cells are likely to be

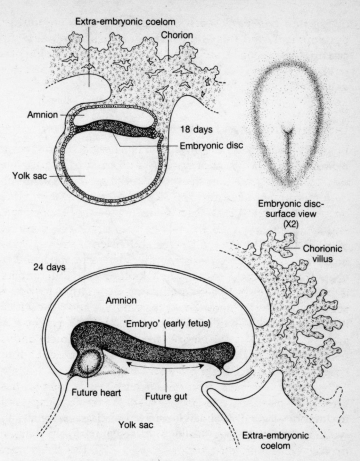

Fig. 1.7 Further embryonic development. The diagrams are enlarged about 90 times from actual (life) size.

needed to form the larger number. From this stage on, the cells, and later the tissues, that are developing into *fetus* (Fig. 1.8; later stages in Figs 2.16 and 2.17) are increasingly easily distinguished from the rest of the *embryo*, which henceforth is more and more obviously being transformed into placenta, fetal membranes, etc. Initially the cells representing the

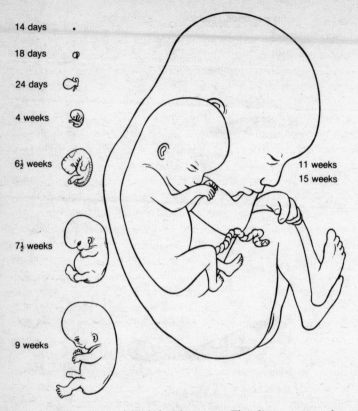

14 days

18 days

24 days

4 weeks

6½ weeks

7½ weeks

9 weeks

11 weeks
15 weeks

Fig. 1.8 Early stages of fetal development. The diagrams are about three-quarters actual (life) size. (From ref. 9.)

future fetus amount to a very small fraction of the total conceptus, but as pregnancy proceeds these relations are reversed, so that at the time of birth the fetus is much greater in bulk than the placenta, etc., soon to be discarded as 'after-birth'.

The derivation of the fetus from the embryo is a remarkable process, and is important because for many people the fetus is much more easily identified as a future person than is the embryo—the transformation has ethical implications, so we should look into the details with some care. Probably, most people unfamiliar with this field would think of the changes as being a continuous line of descent—egg to embryo to fetus to child, each stage being the *full* successor of the one before —but that is not in fact the case. The whole egg certainly becomes the embryo, and the whole fetus becomes the child, but the whole embryo *does not* become the fetus—only *a small fraction* of the embryo is thus involved, the rest of it continuing as the placenta and other auxilliary structures. In addition, the same small fraction of the embryo can become two fetuses, or three, or four, or even more, in the process of 'twinning'. It is important to emphasize that there is a confusion of terms here, which has so often been overlooked; it is attributable to the *traditional* viewpoint, which was current before detailed knowledge was available on just how development of the new individual took place. Some writers, like Anne McLaren,[10,11] have contrived to remedy this by referring to the entity that exists up to the formation of the embryonic disc as a 'pre-embryo' or 'proembryo', and the entity that continues from there on as an 'embryo', later to become the fetus. This device does preserve current nomenclature, by which it is an embryo that becomes a fetus, but really a more logical step would be to think in terms of the embryo continuing, after disc formation, as the placenta, etc., and the fetus arising as *an offshoot* of the embryo. The two different viewpoints can be depicted thus:

Traditional: Egg → embryo → fetus → child
                      ↓
                placenta, etc.

Logical: Egg → embryo → placenta, etc.
               ↓
           fetus → child

Almost the whole of the embryo *manifestly* develops into the placenta, etc., and no-one can deny that, with only a small fraction becoming (eventually) the fetus (Figs 1.5–1.7). So the sequence can be stated rationally as follows: a very small part of the ovary (an oocyte, in fact) becomes an embryo, and a very small part of the embryo (the disc or plate) becomes the fetus. The inference is clear: the embryo should be regarded as an organ, like the ovary, and as such is not entitled to the respect due to something destined to become a person. The embryonic and fetal parts are easily distinguished, a notable fact being that the fetal component grows much faster than the embryo–placental component (Table 1.1 and Fig. 1.9).

A difficulty in accepting this 'logical' viewpoint is the gradualness of the developmental changes. The embryonic disc appears at around the fourteenth day, marking the start of the 'fetal period', but when can the products be called a 'fetus'? A common dictionary definition states that the object (unfortunately still called an embryo) 'becomes' a fetus when its appearance can be recognized as similar to that of the fully developed animal, which leaves plenty of room for an active imagination. In terms of actual periods, *Black's Medical Dictionary* states that it is a fetus after the middle of the second

Table 1.1. Weights of the embryo and its derivatives, including the placenta, and of the fetus and its precursors from the embryonic disc

Weeks of pregnancy[a]	Embryo	Fetus
2	2 mg	3 μg
6	10 g	180 mg
10	20 g	5 g
20	170 g	300 g
40	650 g	3300 g

[a]Values for 2 and 6 weeks of pregnancy estimated from linear measurements of illustrations, remainder from Rhodes.[12]

month (say 6–7 weeks), while *Gray's Anatomy* and the *Concise Oxford* prefer from the end of the 8th week, the *Encyclopaedia Britannica* gives it as about the end of the 9th week, and *Webster's Dictionary* and Arey's *Developmental Anatomy* agree that it is from 3 months onwards (13 weeks plus). Not only that, but those who support the present nomenclature must live with the concept of an embryo originating as a very small

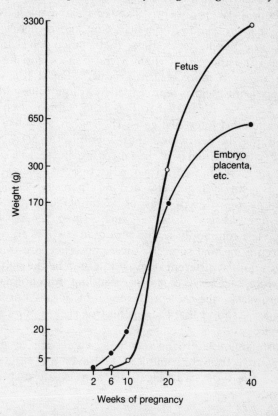

Fig. 1.9 A graph comparing the rates of growth of the embryo and its derivatives, and the fetus. The vertical scale is logarithmic, which tends to obscure the fact that the fetus grows nearly ten times faster than the embryo (later—placenta, fetal membranes, etc.).

part of an embryo! By an alternative system, an embryo originates as a very small part of a pre-embryo, and coexists with the pre-embryo as the latter differentiates into placenta, etc., prior to the embryo 'becoming' a fetus.

Conjoined twins

Sometimes the twinning process goes awry and 'conjoined' or 'Siamese' twins are born. They can take many forms, from those that are almost separate, being joined merely by skin and connective tissue, to those that share a pelvis and a pair of legs, and those that share a chest, neck and head, and there are even more bizarre products (Fig. 1.10). In some instances, one 'twin' is represented by a diminutive and incomplete body, as illustrated in Fig. 1.10f, which often lacks a heart and other internal organs. Then again, a small deformed 'infant' may be discovered entirely within the body cavity of its otherwise normal twin. Instances are on record also where there are mere limbs, an arm or a leg, or even smaller portions such as a single finger, attached as a 'parasite'. Finally there are numerous descriptions of accumulations ('teratomas') consisting of assorted tissues, such as hair, teeth, skin, and bone, etc., commonly within an organ such as an ovary, of apparently normal subjects; these, however, are considered to have quite a different origin and not to be the nether end, as it were, of a series of stages extending from normal twins. Nevertheless, the accepted range of forms encountered adequately shows that there is no true cut-off point for individuality.

Most conjoined twins fail to survive birth or die soon afterwards, though some can be saved by surgery, and others, like type (a) in Fig. 1.10, may live to maturity and beyond.

Deaths in embryos and fetuses

In all mammals that have been investigated, there is evidence that one or more embryos or fetuses are lost during the

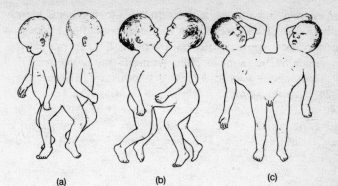

Fig. 1.10 Conjoined twins. (From refs 9 and 13.)

course of pregnancy, even in healthy subjects under the most favourable environmental conditions.[14] Losses in human beings occur generally quite early in pregnancy, the woman often being unaware that she was pregnant. These instances are discovered by means of blood hormone assays: in one study 43 per cent of the women examined showed increases in blood progesterone levels, indicating that implantation had taken place, but shortly afterwards they came into menstruation, which signified that an embryo was no longer present. At this stage of pregnancy, the loss of an embryo is scarcely recognizable as an abortion, the embryo being simply flushed out of the uterus by the menstrual flow. Obvious abortions of a spontaneous nature occur later in pregnancy, and are more frequent in older women: one study recorded 120 spontaneous abortions for every thousand pregnancies in 20–24-year-old women, rising to 280 per thousand in women of 40 or more; in another study, 62 per cent of women lost their conceptuses before the 12th week.[15] (Investigation of embryos initiated in an IVF programme showed that 23 per cent had chromosome abnormalities.)[16,17]

The causes of embryonic and fetal death have been the subjects of much debate and research, and the main reasons are considered to be errors in the number of chromosomes, and other congenital and hereditary defects (see Chapter 2, p. 61), incompatibility between mother and fetus as in 'rhesus disease' (the Rh problem), faults in the maternal hormone system, and sundry infections, particularly those due to the mumps virus and the like.

When does a person's life really begin?

This is the key issue in debates on embryo experimentation. Probably most people who were asked this question would answer 'at fertilization' (or 'conception'). Certainly, several interesting and unusual things happen then (see this chapter, p. 7)—it is really the most *obvious* event to pick—but for biologists the preceding and succeeding cellular processes are *equally* important (see Table 1.2). Nevertheless, 'fertilization' continues to be the cry of many religious bodies and indeed also of the august World Medical Association, who, in 1949, adopted the Geneva Convention Code of Medical Ethics, which contains the clause: 'I will maintain the utmost respect for human life from the time of conception'. So we do need to look more closely at this choice, for a generally acceptable 'beginning' for human life would be a great help in reaching ethical and legal concensus.

In the first place human *life*, as such, obviously begins

before fertilization, since the egg or oocyte is alive before sperm entry, as were innumerable antecedent cells, back through the origin of species into the mists of time. A more practical starting point would be that of the life of the human *individual*, so it is individuality that we should be looking for, at least as one of the essential criteria. Now the earliest antecedents of the eggs, as of sperm, are the primordial germ cells, which can be seen as a group of distinctive little entities migrating through the tissues of the early embryo. When they first become recognizable, they number only about a dozen or two, but they multiply fast and soon achieve large numbers, reaching a peak of 7–10 million about 6 months after conception (Table 1.2 and Fig. 1.11). Then, despite continued active cell division, there is a dramatic decline in the cell population, which has tempted people to suggest that some sort of 'selection of the fittest' occurs, but there is no good evidence in support of this idea; nor is there any good reason to look for individuality in that mercurial population. In due course, the primordial germ cells, while still undergoing cell divisions, settle down in the tissues of the future ovary, change subtly in their characteristics, and thus become oogonia; and then, soon after birth, *cell division ceases*, the cells develop large nuclei and are now recognizable as primary oocytes (Fig. 1.12). From now on, there are steady cell losses but no further cell divisions (except for the polar body extrusions that occur just before ovulation and immediately after sperm penetration); it is the same entity that was a primary oocyte, becomes a fertilized egg, and then develops as an embryo (Fig. 1.13). The primary oocytes are very unusual cells, for they have the capacity to live for much longer than most other body cells; the *same* oocytes can be seen in the ovaries of women approaching the menopause—cells that have lived for about 40 years or longer. And it is with the emergence of the primary oocytes that we can hail the start of *individuality*. Then, in those oocytes that are about to be ovulated, the first meiotic division takes place—another important step, for the 'shuffling' of genes that occurs at that point

Table 1.2. Stages at which the life of 'a person' could begin

Developmental stage	Activity	Significance for 'start of life'	Approximate numbers
Primordial germ cells; oogonia	Successive divisions	Earliest generative cells	5–10 million[a]
Primary oocytes	Cell growth — no division	Origin of individuality	Up to hundreds of thousands[b]
Emission of first polar body	First meiosis; ovulation	Genetic uniqueness established	About 500[c]
Secondary oocyte	Fertilization; second meiosis	Activation; has paternal genes	About 100[d]
Cleavage embryo	Cell division	Potential plurality	80[e]
Blastocyst	Implantation	First maternal response	60
Embryonic disc — neural folds	Primordium of fetus	Logical period for soul entry	30
Day 21 embryo	First heart beat	First 'sign of life'	30
5–6-Week embryo	Nerve reflex possible	Responsiveness	25
Fetus at 12 weeks	Electrical activity — brain	Clinical match for end of life	15
Fetus at 4–5 months	'Quickening'	First 'awareness' by mother	10
Infant	Born and surviving	Full legal status	5[f]

[a] Data from a published count (Fig. 1.11).
[b] See Fig. 1.11.
[c] Based on the calculation that with a fertile life of 40 years an 'average' woman would have about 480 menstrual cycles in which an average of 1.1 eggs would be ovulated: total 528 or say 500.
[d] A fertilization rate of 20 per cent overall seems reasonable, since intercourse would often occur too early or too late for successful fertilization; and some allowance is made for the use of contraceptives.
[e] This and the next six figures are broad estimates, with some basis on published data for early loss rates.
[f] This figure is based on the assumption that the world average starting family would be about five, after allowing for perinatal deaths.

(see p. 5) bestows *genetic uniqueness* on the oocyte. So both individuality and genetic uniqueness are established before sperm penetration and fertilization; these processes have distinctly different actions—providing the stimulus that initiates cleavage and contributing to biparental inheritance. Thus, the preferred choice for the start of the human individual should surely be the formation of the primary oocyte, but there is certaintly no unanimity on this score.

Passing over now the popularity of fertilization, for many people it is instead the emergence of the embryonic disc and primitive streak that most appeals as the stage in which to identify the start of 'personhood' (one or more persons, in view of the imminent possibility of twinning), and there is

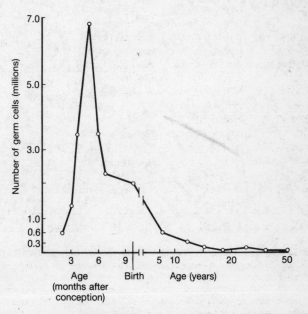

Fig. 1.11 Total numbers of germ cells (primordial germ cells, oogonia, and primary oocytes) in the ovary during life, showing the enormous increase and then diminution in numbers as time passes (see also Table 1.2). (From ref. 18.)

Fig. 1.12 A section of the ovary of a child, showing large numbers of
primary oocytes. (×400)

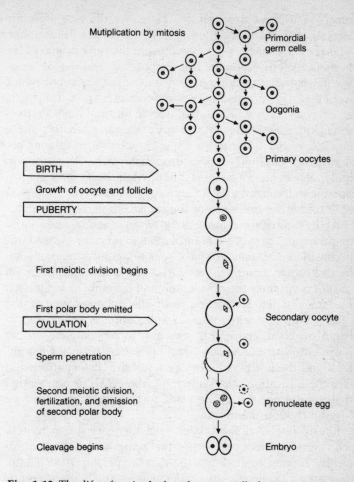

Multiplication by mitosis

Primordial germ cells

Oogonia

Primary oocytes

BIRTH

Growth of oocyte and follicle

PUBERTY

First meiotic division begins

First polar body emitted

OVULATION

Secondary oocyte

Sperm penetration

Second meiotic division, fertilization, and emission of second polar body

Pronucleate egg

Cleavage begins

Embryo

Fig. 1.13 The life of a single female germ cell, from its origin as a primordial germ cell. The vast majority of primordial germ cells, oogonia, and primary oocytes degenerate and disappear before birth (see also Table 1.2). (From ref. 18.)

much to support this opinion. Here, for the first time, are structures that are designed to have a different destiny than *all the rest of the embryo*—they represent the primordium of the fetus (as already described on pp. 14–20), and the developmental patterns of embryo and fetus progressively diverge from this stage onwards. An additional point is that this new emergence is not inevitable, for in around one in two-thousand pregnancies the embryo grows, often to quite a large size, but there is no fetus; the clinical conditions are known as blighted ovum, dropsical ovum, hydatidiform mole, etc. Evidence suggests that hydatidiform mole is attributable to fertilization of a faulty egg, the embryo developing only under the influence of the sperm chromosomes.

At the time of appearance of the embryonic disc, and shortly beforehand, the process of implantation is occurring, and this is considered by many to have special significance in relation to embryonic potential—so far as we know, implantation cannot occur once the development of the embryo has passed the stage when interaction with the endometrium of the uterus normally takes place. Implantation is considered to begin on about the eighth day and to be complete on the fourteenth, or thereabouts, and both the Warnock Committee[19] and the Ethics Advisory Board of the US Department of Health, Education and Welfare (4 May 1979) recommended that no attempt should be made to culture embryos *in vitro* beyond the fourteenth day.

But despite all that has been said, there are still many folk who remain unconvinced—is the being at this stage sufficiently 'human' to qualify as the start of a person? After all, the disc is just a collection of similar cells, virtually undifferentiated, poorly delineated from its surroundings, about a fifth of a millimetre long, non-sentient, and without the power of movement. It is in no way a 'body' and it does not bear the faintest resemblance to a human being—*and* the soul cannot enter yet, for the disc may yet divide in the process of twinning, and the soul being unique is indivisible. Also, it is argued that we should be looking for some spark of personality, and a moral philosopher has proposed that some sort of 'responsiveness' is an essential feature.[20]

One of the earliest succeeding changes in the direction of humanness could be the development of the heart primordium, and soon after that the beginnings of a circulatory system; the first contractions of the heart muscle occur possibly as early as day 21, with a simple tubular heart at that stage, and in the fourth week a functional circulation begins. With the heart beats we have the first movements initiated within the embryo (?fetus) and thus in a way the first real 'sign of life'. The conceptus is now about 6 mm long. During the fifth and sixth weeks, nerve fibres grow out from the spinal cord and make contact with muscles, so that at this time or soon afterwards, a mechanical or electrical stimulus might elicit a muscle twitch; this is important for it would be the first indication of sentient existence—of 'responsiveness'. At this stage, too, the embryo could possibly feel pain. But, still, some would find cause to demur: only an expert could tell that this embryo/fetus, now 12–13 mm in length, with branchial arches (corresponding to the 'gill-slits' in non-mammalian embryos), stubby limbs, and a prominent tail, is human (Fig. 1.14). A marginally more acceptable applicant is the fetus at 7½ weeks, when the hands and feet can be seen to have fingers and toes (Fig. 1.8), and thereafter physical resemblance steadily improves; also at this time, a special gene on the Y-chromosome (the 'testis-determining factor' or TDF) is switched on, and the fetuses that have this chromosome, the males, proceed thenceforward to develop *as* males, distinguishable from females.

At about 12 weeks, electrical activity can be detected in the brain of the fetus, which could signal the dawn of consciousness. Here, we would seem to have a very logical stage marking the *start* of a person, for the cessation of electrical activity in the brain ('brain death') is accepted in both medical and legal circles as marking the *termination* of a person—as an indication that life no longer exists in victims of accidents or in patients with terminal illnesses. Around the fourth or fifth

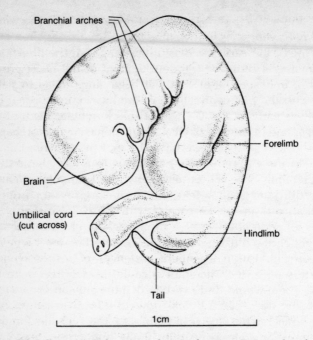

Fig. 1.14 A human 'embryo' (or, better, fetus) at 5–6 weeks of age. (Composite from several sources.)

month of pregnancy, the mother first experiences movements of the fetus ('quickening'), which were regarded by St Thomas Aquinas as the first indication of life, for he believed that life was distinguished by two features, knowledge and movement; moreover, it would seem logical that the fetus would move when the *animus* (life or soul) took up residence.†[21] Before St Thomas, there had been no clear statement of the time of animation; that it had to be a significant period into pregnancy was an inference drawn from an interpretation of *Exodus* xxi, 22–23, but many, like St Augustine, held the view that the soul had to be inherited in the act of

†The modern equivalent would be at about day 21, when the heart begins to beat.

generation—in its tainted form, consistently with the doctrine of Original Sin—yet he himself had made a distinction between *embryo informatus*, before the entry of the soul, when inducing abortion could be considered a minor crime, and *embryo formatus*, when to cause abortion was punishable by death. In the Roman period and at later dates, the time of *formatus* (or *animatus*) was even thought to be different for the two sexes: the fortieth day for the male fetus and the eightieth for the female fetus.

At about 24 weeks, the fetus reaches a state in which it can commonly survive outside the maternal body, with assistance, and at 28 weeks it achieves protection in England under the Infant Life Preservation Act of 1929. Just which stage marks the start of a person's life is a matter of personal opinion. Much of the foregoing argumentation may seem to some people difficult to comprehend, especially if they have not had formal training in biology, and to others may even seem irrelevant, in view of the firm line taken by many church authorities. But it really is important that we should try to reach a concensus on just when a person's life should be held to begin, for the decision does have important practical consequences—it directly affects the rights of other embryos, of fetuses, and of people, as discussed later in Chapter 5, p. 109. (As a further guide, the subject of the moral status of embryos is dealt with very efficiently in ref. 22.)

2

Variations on the theme

Fertilizing eggs and growing and transferring embryos

We discuss here the fertilization in the laboratory (*in vitro*) of mammalian eggs, followed by the transfer of the embryos to the recipient females (put together, this is referred to as IVF+ET). This section is concerned with the research aspects of the work in laboratory animals and human beings (for further information see refs 23–25); the clinical side is dealt with in Chapter 4, pp. 93–101.

The starting point for this line of endeavour came in 1891, when Walter Heape announced that he had been able to transfer embryos between two rabbits and then observe the birth of the young (Table 2.1). He took the precaution of using animals of different strains, so there was no doubt that the young born were derived from the transferred embryos. About the same time, people were trying to fertilize mammalian eggs *in vitro* but with no success. It was certainly tantalizing, in view of the ease with which the eggs of sea urchins, fish, and frogs could be fertilized simply by adding sperm to them, and there were many failures and imagined successes—and this was the situation for some 60 years! Then, in 1954, a group in Paris announced that they had indeed been able to turn the trick with rabbit eggs, but they were content with fertilization alone, being interested in the cytological details of that process. So it was Chang in the USA who became the first person to report the fertilization of mammalian eggs, culture of the resulting embryos, and the birth of young, all in the rabbit. That was in 1959, but it was a few years before anyone could claim to have done the same thing with other animals' eggs—of particular value here would have been the

Table 2.1. Major advances in the development of IVF+ET, and the people announcing them first

1891	First transfer of embryos between animals with subsequent birth of young (rabbit).[a]
1942	First transfer of embryos with birth of young (mouse).[b]
1947	First culture of embryos, followed by transfer to recipients and birth of young (rabbits).[c]
1958	First culture of embryos, followed by transfer to recipients and birth of young (mouse).[d]
1959	First IVF+ET (rabbit).[e]
1970	First IVF+ET (mouse).
1971	First cryopreservation of embryos, followed by transfer to recipients and birth of young (mouse).[g]
1977	First cryopreservation of oocytes, followed by maturation, IVF+ET, and birth (mouse).[h]
1978	First IVF+ET and birth (Man).[i]
1985	First cryopreservation of embryos fertilized *in vitro*, followed by transfer and birth (Man).[j]
1986	First cryopreservation of oocytes, followed by maturation, IVF+ET, and birth (Man).[k]

[a]W. Heape. *Proceedings of the Royal Society* **48**, 457–8.
[b]E. Fekete and C.C. Little. *Cancer Research* **2**, 525–30.
[c]M.C. Chang. *Nature* **159**, 602.
[d]A. McLaren and J.D. Biggers. *Nature* **182**, 877–8.
[e]M.C. Chang. *Nature* **184**, 466.
[f]A.B. Mukherjee and M.M. Cohen. *Nature* **228**, 472–3.
[g]D.G. Whittingham. *Nature* **233**, 125–6.
[h]D.G. Whittingham. *Journal of Reproduction and Fertility* **49**, 89–94.
[i]P.C. Steptoe and R.G. Edwards. *Lancet* **ii**, 366.
[j]J. Cohen, R.F. Simons, C.B. Fehilly, R.G. Edwards, J. Hewitt, G.F. Rowland, P.C. Steptoe and S.M. Webster. *Lancet* **i**, 647. (Priority could possibly belong instead to G.H. Zeilmaker, A.Th. Alberda, I. van Gent, C.M.P.M. Rijkmans and A.C. Drogendijk. *Fertility and Sterility* **2**, 293–6 (1984).[48])
[k]C. Chen. *Lancet* **i**, 884–6.

eggs of mice and rats as the preferred experimental animals, but these proved much less cooperative than rabbit eggs. Determined efforts paid off, however, and during the 1950s means were devised for growing mouse embryos in culture and transferring these to recipients (Table 2.1). By 1970, the whole process from fertilization *in vitro*, to transfer of embryos to recipients, to the birth of young, had been achieved.

The mouse work turned out to be very helpful, because the requisite conditions for success proved to be broadly similar to those needed for fertilizing human eggs *in vitro* and for culturing the embryos. But inevitably there were numerous minor differences, and much time and effort had to be expended before Bob Edwards in the UK was able to report in 1969 the successful fertilization of human eggs *in vitro* and in 1970 their ensuing cleavage in culture. Then followed a tremendous effort to establish methods to fit this manoeuvre into the human clinical situation.

An early problem was how best to obtain eggs from a female patient, and how to ensure that these eggs were in the right state of ripening so that fertilization would occur readily and in a normal manner. Fortunately, at about this time, Edwards came to know Patrick Steptoe, a gynaeocologist specializing in laparoscopy (Fig. 2.1) and working at Oldham General Hospital in Lancashire. A laparoscope is a kind of slim telescope, one end of which can be passed through a small incision in the abdominal wall, enabling the operator to get a clear view of details inside the abdomen. Glass-fibre optics in the laparoscope and a powerful light source ensure good illumination. Various operations can then be done, without having to open up the abdomen, by inserting other specialized instruments through the abdominal wall. The best time to obtain eggs turned out to be just before they are released from the ovary and still within the compartments (follicles) in which they grow. So the eggs were obtained by means of a long needle attached to a hypodermic syringe and inserted into any mature ovarian follicles that had responded to the hormone treatment previously administered to the patient, the proceedings being monitored through the laparoscope. Follicle contents, including the eggs, were drawn up through the needle by gentle suction, and deposited in a small plastic dish. After the addition of sperm and a spell in

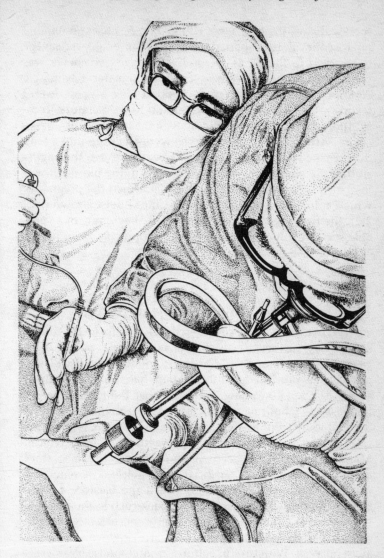

Fig. 2.1 Patrick Steptoe, with Jean Purdy assisting, recovering oocytes from follicles with the aid of a laparascope and a long hypodermic needle. (Original photo by courtesy of Bob Edwards.)

the incubator, the eggs were checked for fertilization under a microscope. Further periods of incubation enabled cleavage to proceed to the 2-, 4-, 8-, or 16-cell stage, whichever was considered likely to give best results on transfer. Favourable conditions for culture were only found after a good deal of testing—they require special attention to temperature, composition of culture medium and even make-up of the atmosphere. After culture, the embryos were taken up into a long thin plastic tube, which could be passed through the vagina so that the embryos could be deposited in the uterus. It was just such a procedure as this that established the pregnancy which culminated in 1978 in the birth of Louise Brown (Fig. 2.2), the first-ever test-tube baby[26]—the beginning of a veritable social revolution! For further developments, see Chapter 4, pp. 93–101.

How far can we grow embryos in culture?

As yet, we have only considered culture up to the 16-cell stage, but further development is possible under these circumstances, though not as a continuous process. Blastocysts can be produced and these often 'hatch' and go through some additional swelling, but after that things tend to get increasingly abnormal. It is, of course, at this stage that implantation would occur, and the impression is that this relationship with the uterine endometrium is truly critical. Many attempts have been made to devise (for laboratory animals' embryos) an 'artificial endometrium'—something resembling the real thing, into which the blastocyst could burrow and in which it could start constructing the placenta to enable it to obtain the necessary nutrients and oxygen, and dispose of carbon dioxide and other waste products. But so far, all to no avail. With careful culture, rat and mouse blastocysts will sometimes grow larger, spread out on the surface of the culture dish, and begin to produce some of the structures characteristic of later normal development. These include,

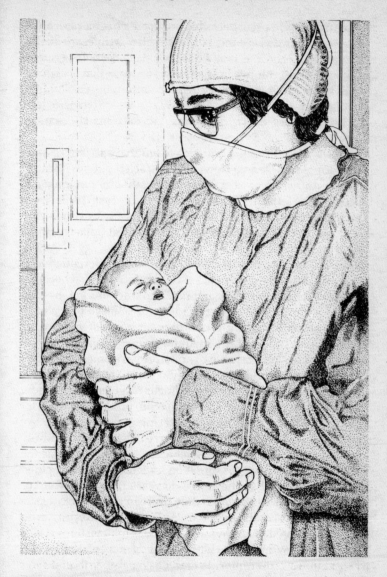

Fig. 2.2 Bob Edwards holding Louise Brown, the first test-tube baby. (Original photo by courtesy of Bob Edwards.)

most strikingly, a small pulsating organ which is the forerunner of the heart, and also some of the 'somites', which are distinctive gatherings of cells that would normally become segments of the vertebral column in later embryos. And that is about as far as it has proved possible to go in continuous culture from the blastocyst stage—still a long way from 'ectogenesis' and the baby factory of the *Brave New World*! (This is discussed further in Chapter 5, pp. 115–22.)

A somewhat different approach to embryo and fetus culture was adopted by Dennis New, who dissected out ('explanted') embryos at various stages after implantation in rats and mice.[27] Soon after implantation, the blastocyst displays the new formation of several different types of cells which later will form different parts of the placenta and adjacent structures, and at this stage it is referred to as an 'egg cylinder', rather an apt descriptive name. This early differentiation is evidently dependent upon the close relationship that becomes established between the embryo and the uterine tissues. Having achieved that differentiation, the embryo is in a position to develop quite a bit further after transfer from the uterine tissues to a culture medium. Dennis New found that such embryos were capable of an impressive amount of additional growth under the conditions of artificial culture. Embryos explanted at the egg cylinder stage and kept under rather special culture conditions could proceed *in vitro* for about 4.5 days, or nearly a quarter of the whole period of pregnancy. During this time, their size increased enormously and distinct anatomical features became evident, such as the limb buds (Fig. 2.3). Explantation at later stages permitted further progress, but the range decreased, so that embryos explanted at 13.5 days would only proceed normally to a state equivalent to 14.5 days (Fig. 2.4). The great difficulty with fetuses explanted at 12 days and later was to devise apparatus that would provide them with sufficient oxygen, and effectively remove carbon dioxide and wastes, rather than deliver sufficient nutrients. A miniature version of the 'Klung system', as described in Chapter 5 (pp. 119–20) for human fetuses

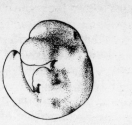

Fig. 2.3 left: rat embryos at the 'egg cylinder' stage, just dissected from the uterus; right: embryos cultured for 4 days from the egg cylinder stage. (From ref. 28.)

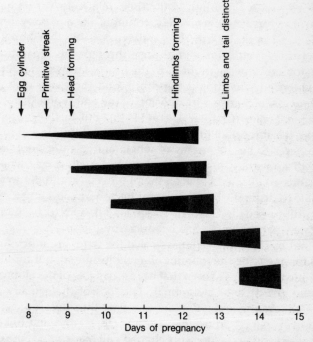

Fig. 2.4 The periods for which rat embryos and fetuses can be grown in culture are indicated by the lengths of the black wedges, the widths of which are roughly proportional to sizes of conceptuses. (From ref. 27.) (Pregnancy in the rat lasts 20–22 days.)

would perhaps be the answer, if the technology could be mastered.

In rats, mice, and rabbits, the 2-, 4-, and 8-cell embryos have remarkable developmental flexibility. If the zona of a 2-cell embryo is removed, the cells will continue to multiply in a culture medium and spread out as a disorganized group. If the individual cells of a 2-cell embryo are placed in two separate zonas, they are each capable of full development, producing thus identical twins. Being within a zona is critical. Similarly, the individual blastomeres of a 4-cell embryo, dealt with in the same way, are each capable of developing into a whole normal animal. The same goes for the blastomeres of the 8-cell embryo, though, with their relatively very small quota of cytoplasm, they rarely continue far and very few succeed in reaching birth. It is indeed possible that human twins (triplets, etc.) sometimes arise through the separation of blastomeres, owing perhaps to the loss of faulty zonas, but the evidence is that this is very rare, and the usual way in which twins, etc. arise is by division of the embryonic disc, as described earlier (Chapter 1, pp. 14–15). But in the present context, it is important to note that the capability of individual blastomeres to be the origins of whole animals does not last long, disappearing just before the blastocyst stage, when adhesions are formed between the outer cells and it becomes possible to distinguish between trophectoderm and inner cell mass (discussed in Chapter 1, pp. 11–13). Or, to be more accurate, that capability has been lost by the trophectoderm cells, not by the inner cell mass cells; the latter are much too small for one to be the founder of a whole animal, but careful experimentation has shown that each is capable of developing into *any part* of the new animal. The loss of that quality is called 'differentiation'—the fate of cells is thus decided, generally irreversibly. So trophectoderm cells are the first to become differentiated; soon this change will overcome some of the cells of the inner cell mass, until eventually all the cells will have their fate sealed.

Further evidence of the adaptability of early embryos is

seen in their tolerance to being bisected, they then proceed as if they were two separate but complete embryos. This can be done at the 16- or 32-cell stages (after cell-to-cell attachment), or at the blastocyst stage. With both forms, recovery from the assault is rapid, and it does not take long for the two halves to possess virtually the developmental potential of the original whole. In the cattle-breeding industry, embryo transfer is very big business—low quality cows can thus carry to birth calves from prize-winning parents. Roughly a quarter of a million are now being transferred annually world-wide, and the use of half-embryos is common.

Producing chimeras and hybrids

Before differentiation occurs in embryos, there is full adaptability, and this means that cells of separate animals (of the same species), taken during the embryonic cleavage stages and before differentiation, and put together in one zona, can develop into a single whole individual animal.[29-31] The result is called a 'chimera', from the mythical monsters of mixed physique. Experimental chimeras in rats and mice generally look perfectly normal, with only a variegated coat pattern reflecting their origin from parents with uniform black or white coats (Fig. 2.5); they have proved very informative in fundamental studies. One finding of interest is that if the original embryos were male and female, the chimera nearly always developed as a male, supporting the conclusion from other work that the male sex tissues develop before the female and so are able to take over control—a point that helps us to understand some of the problems of human intersexuality. Making chimeras (including by injection of cells into the cavity of blastocysts—first done in 1968)[32] can have a valuable practical side too, because one component can sometimes compensate for shortcomings in the other, notably through the sharing of diffusible products, such as hormones. Parthenogenetic cells established as part of a chimera can participate in full normal development (see this chapter pp. 44-5).

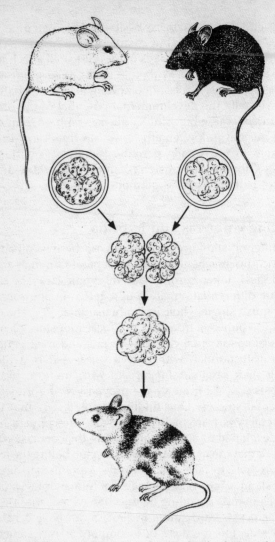

Fig. 2.5 The formation of a mouse chimera by the fusion of embryos from a white and a black mouse.

Even cancer cells can be 'tamed' by incorporation in a chimera.[33] The potential value of 'ES' cells (this chapter, pp. 58–9 and 82–4) rests on the same mechanism. The device might prove valuable as an alternative to genetic engineering for correcting deficiencies in genetically defective human embryos and fetuses—and even people.

Chimeras have been produced between different breeds of sheep, and they differ in subtle ways from hybrids between the same breeds; the same has been done with different breeds of cattle, though important practical advantages have yet to emerge. Chimeras between sheep and goats have also been reported.[34,35]

Hybrids are produced through the mating of animals of different species or by cross-insemination,[36] and so are 'biparental', with characters that reflect the influence of the dominant genes of each parent, while most effects are 'averaged' to varying degrees. By contrast, the chimera resulting from the union of two embryos can be biparental, triparental, or tetraparental in its characters: it functions as an integrated organism to the extent that the various genomes can reach a compromise, or can complement each other's influence. Hybrids are known between a number of different species, but the most famous is probably the mule.

If a viable hybrid is to follow the mating or cross-insemination of species, they must generally have about the same chromosome number and structure, some differences being tolerable if they involve the smaller chromosomes; these features are even more important in determining whether the hybrid is to be fertile or sterile, but a great deal of variation is evident.[37] Crosses that have been made between animals like the rabbit and hare, ferret and mink, and sheep and goat can result in quite extensive embryonic development, but no recorded births.[38]

Attempts to obtain cross-fertilization *in vitro* between the gametes of different rodent species have generally yielded a low rate of success, apparently because of the selective nature of the barrier presented by the zona; the frequency increased only somewhat when the zona was removed, so it is inferred that other barriers also exist.[3] The zona-free hamster egg can be fertilized by a human sperm,[39] and this has become an accepted laboratory method for assessing the fertilizing ability of sperm from infertile patients. Eggs thus fertilized can proceed to the 2-cell stage of embryonic development, which represents a marginal form of hybridization.

Fusions between the cells of different animal species can be induced *in vitro*, and the 'somatic cell hybrids' thus obtained between human and mouse cells have proved invaluable in genetic studies. In such cell hybrids, the human chromosomes are progressively lost and this occurs in a random manner; when only one human chromosome is left and the cell is found to be synthesizing a particular enzyme, a reasonable inference is that the gene specifying that enzyme is on that chromosome. By this and related means, many genes have been located.[40]

Parthenogenesis

Reproduction by parthenogenetic means, i.e. without the involvement of fertilization, is well known in honey bees (for 'drone' production) and a number of other insects, and even in some vertebrates—several races of lizards as well as (occasionally) birds, notably the domestic turkey. Cleavage of the egg proceeds spontaneously and there is either no meiosis or just the first meiotic division, the reduced chromosome number then being made good by internal doubling-up. In mammals, a measure of parthenogenesis sometimes occurs spontaneously or after the application of physical or chemical stimuli, with apparently normal development proceeding to about half-way through pregnancy. There have been claims to have induced development in rabbits which resulted in the birth of young. Sadly, this work could not be repeated in other laboratories, and as yet there is no properly substantiated instance of parthenogenetic mammalian young being born. The reasons for the difficulty in obtaining full development is being actively investigated in several institutions. The main factor seems to be that the male and female chromosome complements in mammals each have a specific 'imprint' of their origin, and both complements are necessary for full normal development.[41,42] Having a female but no male component allows limited progress, but having a male but no female component (the female side sometimes degenerates during fertilization, resulting in 'androgenesis') is known in human reproduction to result in the appearance of a 'hydatidiform mole'—in place of a fetus, there is a strange mass of tissue which can become malignant. The failure of parthenogenesis in mammals is, however, rather a mystery, for a chimera formed between a parthenogenetic and a normal embryo can proceed to normal birth and maturity, with cells of parthenogenetic origin not only contributing to the ordinary body tissues but also acting as precursors of fertile germ cells. Clearly, the parthenogenetic state itself does not induce cell lethality. (For further information, see ref. 43.)

Cloning in animals and human beings

If a sample of tissue, such as skin, is placed in culture, cells will grow out from it in a spreading sheet. This assembly will consist of cells of several different kinds, but if individual cells are picked out and recultured separately, all the descendants will have the same genetic constitution (excluding the effects of mutations, which are very rare) as the original selected cell. In this way, a 'clone' of cells (from the Greek word *klon*, meaning 'a twig') is produced, and the possibility has long been envisaged of producing in a similar way clones deriving from selected individual animals or even people— exact copies all showing the prized traits.

In a sense, cloning occurs naturally, in the process of identical twinning; here the armadillos excel, the Texas armadillo *Dasypus novemcinctus* regularly having identical quadruplets, and in a southern species, *D. hybridus*, the litter can consist of eight to twelve identical young. Identical twins are, of course, also well known in human beings. As mentioned earlier, identical twins occur naturally as a result of the sub-division of the primordium of the fetus (Chapter 1, pp. 14–15), but the same result can be achieved artifically by separating the blastomeres of early cleavage embryos (see this chapter, p. 40), and as many as eight identical young rabbits have been produced in this way. To obtain larger numbers, other methods are clearly needed. The most impressive result has been obtained in the frog—this involved taking nuclei from the cells of a tadpole (specifically from cells lining the intestine) and inserting these into eggs that had been irradiated to destroy their nuclei.[44,45] Commonly, subsequent development was very limited, but sometimes it led to the appearance of adult animals (Fig. 2.6). Because of the large numbers of nuclei available, numerous adult frogs could be obtained, all exact genetic copies of the tadpole from which the nuclei had been extracted.

Over the past 30-odd years, numerous attempts have been made to do the same kind of thing with mammals, and occasional claims for success (chiefly in rats and mice) have been heard, the most recent arousing a great deal of interest in 1981–2. Unfortunately, none of these claims could be substantiated by other workers, and the two recent reports were later admitted to have been based on errors. The positive results that have been confirmed in other laboratories were very modest by comparison—to see *any* ensuing embryonic development, it was necessary to take nuclei from 8-cell embryos or from the inner cell mass cells of blastocysts, and place these in eggs undergoing fertilization, from which the pronuclei had been removed. The products advanced through two or three cleavage divisions and then regularly degenerated. The inference drawn was that in mammals the mechanism in nuclei that controls cell function undergoes changes during the course of development appropriate to the successive stages, and cannot revert to an earlier kind of activity. At first, this looked like the end of the trail, but then a further procedure was introduced which revived hopes.

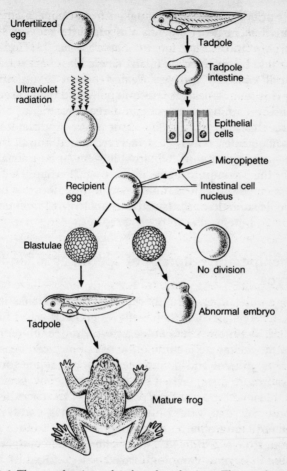

Fig. 2.6 The production of a frog by cloning. The nucleus of an unfertilized egg is destroyed by ultraviolet radiation, and replaced by a nucleus taken from an intestinal cell of a tadpole. A small proportion of the eggs develop into mature frogs. (From ref. 45.)

When nuclei for transfer were taken from cleavage embryos *resulting from* nuclear transfer, the products showed themselves capable of *more extensive development.*[46] (The same result could be obtained by fusing single blastomeres from 8- or 16-cell embryos with enucleated halves of unfertilized eggs.) This 'double-transfer' technique would indeed seem to have made cloning in mammals a real possibility. So far, though, this has only been done with undifferentiated embryonic nuclei, which exist in very limited numbers, and so the mammalian work would still seem to be a long way short of the accomplishments in the frog. (Perhaps, a 'triple-transfer' method would finally open the door? Whether embryonic stem (ES) cells (see this chapter, p. 82) will find an application here is also an open question.)

Low-temperature storage of sperm, eggs, and embryos

The first real progress with the freezing and thawing of sperm, with retention of their fertilizing power, was achieved in the UK in 1950 by Chris Polge and Audrey Smith with bull sperm, the technique including the use of a glycerol-containing semen diluent and a controlled rate of cooling (only to $-79\,°C$ in those days). When the thawed semen was used for artificial insemination, a high proportion of the cows became pregnant. Successful freezing of human sperms, with retention of fertilizing ability, was reported in 1953. Since then, techniques have improved and a better storage temperature of $-196\,°C$ is now commonly used, the refrigerant being liquid nitrogen. Under these circumstances, the period of storage is held to be indefinite, though with a slight loss in fertilizing ability.

The desire to store unfertilized human eggs (ovarian oocytes) in the frozen state reflects a wish to avoid similar storage of embryos, because of the weightier ethical considerations associated with the latter. Success in experimental animals, assessed on the basis of subsequent fertilizability and potential for development into a viable embryo, was achieved first in the mouse in 1977, and was reported also for human oocytes in 1986 (see Table 2.1), but much more still needs to be known about how well human oocytes tolerate the treatment.[47]

Much more attention has been given to the storage of embryos at low temperatures, those of the mouse having been shown in 1971 to be capable of developing to birth after freezing (to −79 °C) and transfer. Success with human embryos (frozen to −196 °C), followed by the birth of normal infants, was perhaps first achieved in 1985 by a group in the UK, though a team in The Netherlands could possibly claim priority[48] (see Table 2.1). Subsequent experience has shown that some 50–70 per cent of human (and monkey) embryos survive freezing to −196 °C.[49]

Storage of embryos at −196 °C (cryopreservation) seems a safe device. Such temperatures are apparently without effect on the genetic properties of cellular systems, but DMSO (the protective agent often used) can apparently de-repress some repressed genetic systems, and so the recommendation is to keep contact of embryos with DMSO to a minimum. Freezing itself is not known to produce any developmental anomalies —this is consistent with the fact that all attempts to induce birth defects by treatments applied to cleavage embryos have been unsuccessful,[50] evidently because all the component cells are 'totipotent' (capable of developing into all parts of the later embryo, including the placenta), and injurious treatment may kill some or all of the cells, but if sufficient numbers remain they can proceed to form a whole embryo. The total freezing (storage) period of embryos is sometimes limited by clinics or statutory authorities to 2–10 years, but this is unimportant for the health of the embryos, for during freezing they are partially protected from ionizing radiations, though the reduced effect does accumulate at a low level. It has been calculated that the mutation rate would be doubled after about 5000 years of storage![48]

The cryopreservation of human embryos presents several

ethical problems, which arise if the parents later disclaim any interest in them (family size completed or parents divorced) or if one or both parents die. Are the embryos to be treated as property or progeny? Commonly, IVF clinics require parents to assign decisions on unwanted or unclaimed embryos to the managers of the clinic, but then these people may in turn be faced with the problem of 'disposal'—for research or donation? If donation, within what time span? One could have children born coeval with the grandchildren of their brothers or sisters, or even later generations. Would this matter very much? If the parents get divorced, what happens to the embryos? It is in fact technically possible to divide them in half!—at least with cattle embryos, in which the procedure is widely used, as transferring two half-embryos has been found to increase the prospects of establishing a pregnancy, but its feasibility and justification with human embryos has yet to be tested. There are clearly opportunities for legal manoeuvres in the matter of unwanted or 'over-wanted' embryos, and in some respects the problems of children arising from donated embryos are similar to those of adopted children.

Genetic engineering

This field of endeavour lies mostly in the future, and its full potential is probably well beyond our present comprehension. But there are many things that can be done now by methods applicable to the test-tube baby procedure, so some thoughts on this topic are well justified. (For useful reviews, see refs 51–64.)

In a strict sense, genetic engineering began with the production of the mule about 3000 years ago, but of course with its present connotation the term refers rather to the highly sophisticated laboratory activity of 'recombinant DNA technology', and this began not very long ago. It probably owes its origin to observations made by Fred Griffith in the UK, who reported in 1928 that some of the heritable characteristics shown by bacteria when they are grown in laboratory culture systems could be exchanged between two strains of the same organism (*Streptococcus pneumoniae*) by means of cell-free extracts, and in 1944 workers at the Rockefeller Institute in the USA established that the 'information' that passed from one strain to the other was, as it were, written into the structure of molecules of DNA (deoxyribonucleic acid). The process is known as 'transformation'. Later, other people in the USA found that viruses were capable of transferring the DNA molecules from one bacterial strain to another, or from one mammalian cell to another, or even between viruses and mammalian cells; this method of information exchange was identified by the names 'transduction' or (later) 'transfection'.

DNA is a chemical compound that can exist in the form of a gigantic molecule of almost indefinite length, which, despite its size, has quite a simple structure. This molecule represents the master code that specifies all the heritable characteristics of the organism. In human beings, there are about six thousand million repetitions of four relatively simple components called 'nucleotides' arranged in line. Amazingly, the *order* in which these nucleotides are set actually 'spells out' the identity of the component units (amino acids) that will make up particular *proteins*. And so, as we pass along the line, we can read out each protein, one after another. This is, in principle, what is done in the cell in the course of protein synthesis. Proteins are the stuff of life, constituting most of the structure of all cells, and they are also the most active elements in cells, taking such forms as enzymes (of which there are untold numbers), oxygen carriers, antibodies, blood-clotting factors, and some hormones. Proteins are responsible for most body functions and control the manufacture, storage, utilization, and disposal of the non-protein components. A group of roughly 1000 nucleotides, acting together for a particular specification, is known as a 'gene', and there are some 50 000 to 100 000 genes in every human tissue cell, arranged neatly, each one in its place, along the DNA chain, which is about 2 m in length. Actually, the chain does not exist as a single structure but as shorter lengths which are tightly coiled and packed into the nucleus in the form of 46 chromosomes (Fig. 2.7). We know the positions of very many genes on the different chromosomes; as an example, the X-chromosome is depicted in Fig. 2.8, with the positions indicated for some 53 genes, though in fact the positions of well over 200 are known. In this way, the specifications for our inheritance are stored, ready to be interpreted by the nuclear machinery for the realization of each character. And it was in fact genes, as bits of a DNA chain, that were transferred between Griffith's bacterial colonies and can be ferried by viruses from cell to cell. The new genes become integrated into the recipient's own genome, so that subsequently both lots of genes are not only functional but also inherited.

The fact that genes free of other cell entities could be transferred between cells was exploited effectively in 1974 by Rudolph Jaenisch and Beatrice Mintz,[67] who found that the distinctive DNA of a virus they selected, when injected into the cavity of a mouse blastocyst, was evidently taken up

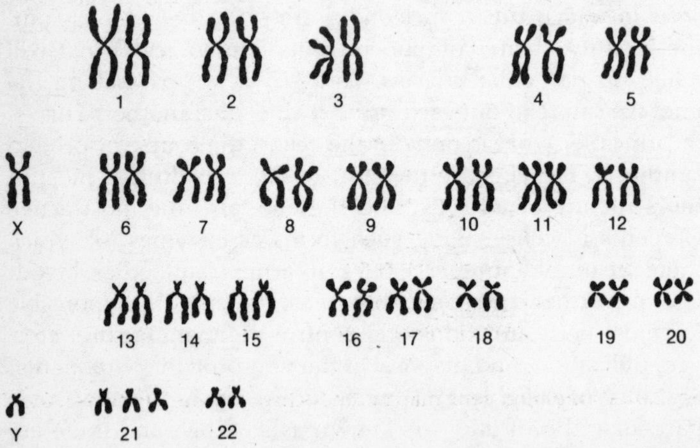

Fig. 2.7 The chromosomes of a Down's syndrome patient, showing the X and Y sex chromosomes, and pairs of all the other chromosomes except no. 21, of which three are present. (From ref. 65.)

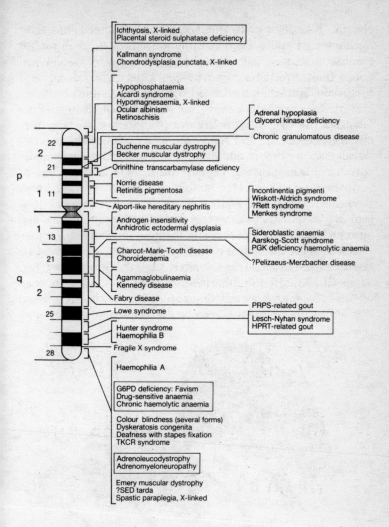

Fig. 2.8 A simplified gene map of the X-chromosome. (From ref. 66.)

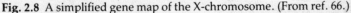

by the blastocyst cells and became incorporated into their
genomes: it could be detected in the tissues of the adult
mouse that eventually developed after the blastocyst had
been transferred to a foster female. Other workers exposed
embryos to infectious viruses ('retroviruses', which have the
ability to contribute directly to the genome of a cell), or
injected the virus into mouse egg pronuclei or into the cavities of blastocysts, and noted the expression of the gene in
adult body tissues; in addition, they observed transmission to
progeny, thus proving genome incorporation. (The use of
viruses for gene transfer is discussed in ref. 68.) A climax
came in 1982, when Richard Palmiter, Ralph Brinster, and
colleagues[69] announced that injection into mouse egg
pronuclei of DNA representing the gene controlling the production of growth hormone in the rat resulted in the eventual
birth of mice that grew much larger than the normal size (Fig.
2.9). (It should be emphasized that the larger than normal
size of the mice was not due specifically to an effect of *rat*
growth hormone, but was because the recipients came to have a

Fig. 2.9 A mouse of much-larger-than-normal size which developed
from a pronucleate egg injected with rat growth hormone genes
(seen here with a litter-mate of normal size). (Based on data in ref. 70.)

supply of growth hormone *additional* to their own.) Observations on the progeny of much-larger-than-normal male mice, when mated with normal-sized females, revealed that the transferred gene had become installed in the reproductive cells and so was heritable (Fig. 2.10).[70,71] The work also showed that the genes had good functional capacity across species boundaries, and this potentiality has been observed also for other genes in other animals by other investigators (Table 2.2).[72,73] The transfer of growth hormone genes in livestock has also been rewarded by increased rates of growth or larger final size in both pigs and sheep; in addition, the ovine growth hormone gene has been isolated and characterized.[74]

Further work by the group responsible for the mouse growth hormone study revealed that the genes appeared to have become incorporated in several different regions of the genome. The likelihood is that the actual location could be important—perhaps even critical—for proper function with some genes, but it is not clear at present how genes could be directed to specific regions (except by 'homologous recom-

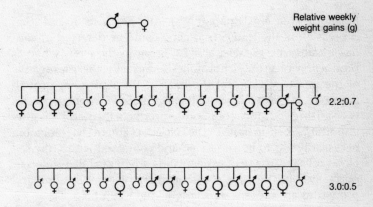

Fig. 2.10 The 'family tree' of a male mouse of much-larger-than-normal size (Fig. 2.9) mated with a female of normal size, showing the transmission of rat growth hormone genes to at least the 'grandchildren'. Mice with the gene made bigger weekly weight gains than those without. (Based on data in ref. 70.)

Table 2.2. Genes transferred to the mouse, with subsequent production of the corresponding gene products

Gene product	Nature of product
Rabbit β-globin	Blood protein
Mouse thymidine kinase	Enzyme involved in DNA synthesis
Rat growth hormone	A pituitary hormone
Human growth hormone	A pituitary hormone
Chicken transferrin	Blood protein
T-antigen	Protein of a cancer cell
Mouse μ light chain (Ig)	A protein of the immune system
Mouse κ heavy chain (Ig)	A protein of the immune system
Rat elastase	A protein-digesting enzyme
Product of the *myc* gene	Protein of a cancer cell
Rat myosin light chain	A protein of muscle tissue
Alphafetoprotein	An important blood protein in the fetus
Human β-globin	Blood protein

Based on ref. 73.

bination'—see next paragraph). It was also found that expression of the transferred gene could be detected in various tissues, the greatest activity being in the liver, whereas production of growth hormone is normally the prerogative of the pituitary gland at the base of the brain. For growth hormone, it may well be of little significance where synthesis is occurring, but for other bodily products it could be highly important. For instance, the blood pigment haemoglobin necessarily has to be generated and contained within the red blood cells if carriage of oxygen and carbon dioxide is to occur normally, and haemoglobins of different compositions and properties are present during fetal and adult life.

A partial solution to the problem of gene location has come with the observations on 'homologous recombination'. This was observed when portions of haemoglobin genes were added to human cells in culture and became correctly located without outside help.[75] Progress was also reported by another group who examined lines of mouse embryonic stem cells (ES cells, which are discussed further on pp. 82–3) in order to select those carrying an abnormal version of the gene that normally specifies the enzyme hypoxanthine–guanine phosphoribosyl transferase (HPRT), the lack of which causes Lesch–Nyhan disease in human beings (see this chapter, pp. 66, 68). With the help of a virus, it proved possible to introduce normal HPRT genes (of both mouse and human origins) into the cells, and the new genes achieved the right location through homologous recombination.[76]

The possibility of repairing genetic defects by gene transfer is obviously of special importance, and in this connection, interest attaches to a condition in mice known as the 'shiverer mutation', the animals suffering from an uncontrollable shaking which sends them to an early grave. The fault appears to lie in the absence of a coat normally encasing nerves in the brain and spinal cord, and the lack of a coat is in turn due to the failure of cells to synthesize a particular component, namely 'myelin basic protein' (MBP). When the gene for MBP was injected into the pronuclei of eggs from affected females, one of the resulting mice grew up to be quite normal, and its progeny were healthy too, showing that the normal gene had become functionally integrated into the genome.[77] This work had the additional merit of demonstrating that integration was not prevented by the continuing presence of the abnormal gene. These observations and certain others have supported the idea that substitution of a defective gene is not necessary and that an added normal gene can override the effects of the faulty one.

For the repair of human traits and diseases by means of genetic engineering, the preference very definitely is for the use of methods applicable to the individual after birth, and perhaps also to the late fetus, but not to the preimplantation embryo. This is for several reasons that have emerged from the wide experience with animal embryos. For one thing, the requisite manipulation is quite traumatic and a large proportion of embryos die in consequence. Then, results that have been obtained have been highly variable, ranging from the totally negative to the wholly unpredictable. Also, there are valid reasons for fearing that ill-sited genes would interfere with the normal function of resident genes, even perhaps activating a cell-growth gene so that it becomes a cancer gene. In some experiments involving gene transfer in mice, spontaneous rearrangements of DNA occurred, resulting in the deaths of many embryos soon after implantation.[78] Finally, transferred genes quite frequently become installed in the forerunners of sperm and eggs, i.e. in the 'germline'; this could be advantageous when the effects are beneficial, as with those of the growth hormone gene noted above, but manifestly unwanted when they are deleterious. Under these circumstances, it is important that treatment of human subjects should avoid 'germline therapy' and concentrate on 'somatic cell therapy'.

A start has been made with somatic cell therapy in several laboratories, and one recently reported experiment provides hope for people who are sufferers from any of the several thalassaemias—disorders of haemoglobin production—which as a group constitute the commonest of the genetic diseases. A human haemoglobin gene was introduced with the aid of a virus (i.e. by transfection) into bone marrow tissue extracted from mice, and the treated tissue then returned to the mice, which soon thereafter began producing human haemoglobin.[79,80] Such a procedure would be especially valuable in human medicine because bone marrow could be removed from a thalassaemia patient, treated by incorporating a normal form of the aberrant haemoglobin gene, tested to make sure that things were functioning normally, and then returned to the patient.

Further possibilities could emerge from research currently in progress with experimental animals on cultured ES cells[81] (mentioned above) and other cell lines. As with bone marrow tissue, genes can be inserted into these cells, the results tested for function, and the cells used for therapy. So far, the application has been chiefly to embryos, but prospects for use with late human fetuses and people after birth are improving.

Other aspects of recombinant DNA technology offer a much brighter picture; of immediate value and with exciting potentialities are the DNA 'probes', which make possible the detection of abnormal genes in animal and human embryos, fetuses, and mature individuals, and so have become invaluable in diagnosis.[11,82] Probes are short lengths of DNA (the method can also be applied to RNA) which have been synthesized as exact copies of abnormal genes, and then labelled with a radioactive substance so that they can be discerned easily. When added to an extract of cells from an animal or person carrying an abnormal gene, the probes become attached to the aberrant items, and to nothing else as the reaction is highly specific. The test is so sensitive that it can be done on material from just a few cells, and so is applicable to the testing of embryos and early fetuses. Even greater sensitivity can be conferred by the procedure of 'gene amplification', which can enormously multiply the number of DNA sequences recovered.[83] Finally, probes can be constructed so as to unite with the 'repeat sequences' of DNA that exist on the Y-chromosome, and can thus be used to identify male cells (see also p. 61).

Another new method depends on the finding that everybody's hereditary specification or genome contains a *unique* array of so-called 'hypervariable' regions (unique except in identical twins), which can readily be analysed to establish relationships between embryos, fetuses, children, and people; appropriately, the method is known as 'genetic fingerprinting'.[84,85]

A rather different application of recombinant DNA technology involves synthesis of hormones and other agents. Insulin, formerly extracted laboriously from animal pancreas, is now synthesized in bacteria in large quantities; even more abundant production has been achieved by programmed silkworms.[86] Other hormones and biologically active agents being produced by 'engineered' bacteria include somatostatin (the growth regulator), human growth hormone,[87] erythropoietin (controlling red cell production), factors defective in haemophilia, the 'tissue plasminogen activator' (TPA) (an enzyme produced in the ovarian follicle which seems important for ovulation, and is also invaluable for dissolving clots in blood vessels), interferon (which helps protect body cells from virus invasion), and probably, by now, many more such agents. The gene for TPA, combined with genes controlling certain aspects of milk production, have been introduced into mice with the result that the mouse milk contains TPA.[88]

Ascertaining sex before birth

Efforts are made to find out the sex of the unborn chiefly in order to exclude, if possible, the presence of a sex-linked genetic anomaly (the various forms of which are discussed on pp. 61–71).

Sex can be ascertained by the examination of samples of tissue taken either from the preimplantation embryo or from the postimplantation embryo or fetus. With the preimplantation embryo, work with laboratory and agricultural animals has shown that suitable material can be obtained by removing a blastomere from a 4- or 8-cell embryo, or a few cells from a blastocyst, with little effect on the viability of these embryos. One research group removed samples of cells from the blastocysts of marmosets, and returned the blastocysts after a period in culture; several normal births were later recorded.[89] Application of these methods to human embryos is currently subject to restrictions in most centres, but it is encouraging to learn that a 4-cell human embryo was found after cryopreservation to have only one intact blastomere left, yet it implanted after transfer and initiated an advanced pregnancy.[90] There would indeed be advantages to be gained from the use of these methods with some patients.[91] With the postimplantation conceptus, cells or tissue samples can be obtained by villus biopsy, amniocentesis, or fetoscopy; and in late pregnancy, sex can be recognized from the anatomy of the fetus when examined at 15–20 weeks of pregnancy by ultrasonography, radiography, nuclear magnetic resonance, and feto-scopy (see pp. 72–9).

When cell or tissue samples are available, the sex of the embryo or fetus can be determined by any of the following five procedures:

1. Chromosome analysis: the presence of two X-chromosomes indicates a female, and an X and a Y a male.

2. The presence of the H–Y antigen, which is a protein that is detectable on the surface of cells removed from male animals, with the aid of an immunological test; the protein is specified by a gene on the Y-chromosome.[92,93]

3. Detection of either of two X-linked enzymes: HPRT (hypoxanthine–guanine phosphoribosyl transferase) and G6PD (glucose-6-phosphate dehydrogenase).[94] Female embryos will initially have twice the amount of these enzymes as males, because they have two X-chromosomes. Shortly before implantation, however, one X-chromosome in females is 'inactivated', so this test is no use after that point.

4. Examination of cells for the presence of the 'sex chromatin', a distinctive little body that normally only occurs in cells from female animals, from the blastocyst stage onwards (see Fig. 2.11).

5. Detection of 'Y-specific DNA repeat sequences', which is a genetic engineering technique (see p. 59) depending on on the addition of a specially designed chemical 'probe' to an extract of the cells or tissue; the probe sticks to any repeat sequences present and is easily seen because it has been stained.[95,96]

Congenital and inherited traits and diseases

The word 'congenital' comes from the Latin *congenitus*, meaning 'born with', and is used to distinguish those traits and diseases that are evident at birth but are not directly attribu-

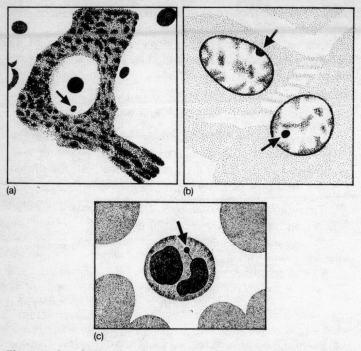

Fig. 2.11 Sex chromatin as it appears in the nuclei of (a) a nerve cell, (b) connective tissue cells, and (c) a white blood cell (leucocyte). (From ref. 59.)

table to the actions of aberrant genes, these being identified as 'inherited'. Congenital defects include those due to visible chromosomal disorders, environmental factors, and unknown agents; the chromosomal errors are relevant for discussion here.

Chromosomal disorders can take several different forms, the more common of which are listed in Table 2.3. The errors can occur in general body cells, when they commonly have very little significance, or in the cells that are the immediate antecedents of the gametes or those that are involved in the fertilization process itself, when they are responsible for ano-

Table 2.3. Frequency of chromosomal errors at birth (data mostly from ref. 52)

Translocations and inversions, etc.[a]	1/80
Monosomies (autosomes)	very rare
Trisomy-21	1/700
Trisomy-18	1/3000
Trisomy-13	1/5000
47,XXY (sex chromosome trisomy) (Klinefelter's syndrome	1/1000 males
47,XYY (sex chromosome trisomy)	1/1000 males
47,XXX (sex chromosome trisomy)	1/1000 females
45,X (monosomy-X) (Turner's syndrome)	1/2500 females
Triploidy	very rare
Tetraploidy	very rare

[a]Including deletions, ring chromosomes, duplications, isochromosomes, centric fragments.

malies in embryos, fetuses, and people. Chromosomes, it appears, are apt to break at any time and then need rejoining; generally this takes place in a normal way, the chromosomes being none the worse for wear, but sometimes repair is faulty, and a rejoined section is put back the wrong way round, producing an 'inversion', or if two or more chromosomes are simultaneously broken, they may be reassembled with parts belonging to others, the results being 'translocations'. In addition, a detached piece of chromosome may be added as an extra bit to a chromosome that already has that piece (a 'duplication') or may simply be 'lost' (a 'deletion'). The frequency of such events is increased by certain agents, such as X-rays or chemicals, with the capacity to induce 'mutations' (mutagenic agents), a term that includes these chromosome changes as well as changes in the structure of genes. Chromosomes may also fail to be moved correctly at cell division; if one gets 'left behind', it becomes responsible for an excess in the group that it should have quitted, as well as a deficiency in the group that it should have joined. Following fertilization (with the other gamete normal), these errors result in 'trisomy' and 'monosomy', respectively.

Trisomy of chromosome number 21 is illustrated in Fig. 2.7 —this is the chromosomal status that distinguishes the clinical condition of 'Down's syndrome' or 'trisomy-21'. Finally, if either the first or second polar body fails to be formed, the egg comes to fertilization with twice as many chromosomes as it should have, and when fertilization proceeds with a normal sperm, the result is a threefold chromosome complement or 'triploidy'. This state also ensues if two sperms fertilize an egg instead of just one; if three sperms get involved, the result is 'tetraploidy'.

Chromosomal errors have drastic consequences for development and nearly all the affected embryos and fetuses suffer spontaneous abortion in the first half of pregnancy (see Table 2.4). The small proportion surviving to birth accounts for anomalies in about 0.6 per cent of infants born, for whom the incidence of specific disorders was shown in Table 2.3. People born with translocations and inversions are generally not noticeably affected themselves, but the consequences for the next generation can be serious, owing to the inevitable disturbance of meiosis. Monosomies and trisomies are uncommon to very rare, except in the case of trisomy-21, mentioned above, the incidence of which is linked to mater-

Table 2.4. Chromosomal status in early spontaneous abortuses (data from ref. 52)

Apparently normal	40 percent
Abnormal	60
trisomy (mostly trisomy-16)[a]	30
45,X	10
triploid	10
tetraploid	5
other	5

[a]The next most frequent were trisomies-15, -21, and -22, with incidences of about 10, 13, and 10 per cent, respectively.

nal age (Fig. 2.12). The sex chromosome monosomies and trisomies provide an exception, in that the individuals affected generally survive to maturity and beyond, but showing various peculiarities of physique, mentality, and fertility. Infants with triploidy and tetraploidy are grossly abnormal and do not survive long.

A distinctive group of *inherited* traits and diseases is composed of the sex-linked conditions (Table 2.5). These involve only the X-chromosome, as the Y-chromosome has very few genes and these, except for the one specifying the H–Y antigen (also known as the 'testis-determining factor' or TDF), have very limited significance. There are well over 200 examples of X-linked traits and diseases. X-linked *dominant*

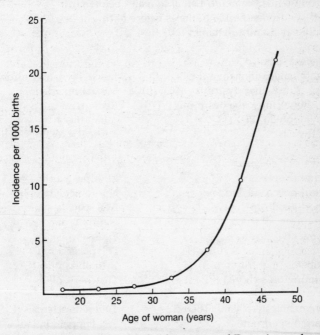

Fig. 2.12 The dramatic rise in the frequency of Down's syndrome births in women who become pregnant when more than 30 years old. (Data from various sources.)

conditions are very rare—odd items like brown discoloration
of the teeth, and a form of rickets resistant to vitamin D, but
also the Rett syndrome, which is lethal to males before birth
and severely limits the life-span of females. X-linked *recessive*
conditions include red–green colour blindness, the Duchenne
and Becker muscular dystrophies (progressive muscular
weakness and death beween 20 and 40 years), the Lesch–
Nyhan syndrome (in the worst forms, the children appear

Table 2.5. Some inherited traits and diseases

X-linked dominant
Brown discolouration of teeth
Incontinentia pigmenti. Lethal to males before birth.
Rett syndrome. Lethal to males before birth.
Rickets resistant to vitamin D

X-linked recessive

Agammaglobulinaemia (PD)	Lesch–Nyhan syndrome
Becker muscular dystrophy (PD) (L)	Mental retardation
Duchenne muscular dystrophy (PD) (L)	Red–green colour
Haemophilia (PD) (T)	blindness
Ichthyosis	Testicular feminization (F)

Autosomal dominant

Achondroplasia	Multiple exostoses (C)
Adult polycystic kidneys	Myotonic dystrophy (PD)
Apert syndrome	Nail–patella syndrome (L)
Blindness	Neurofibromatosis (C)
Congenital deafness	Otosclerosis (T)
Congenital spherocytosis (T)	Polyposis coli (C)
Diabetes (maturity onset) T)	Retinoblastoma (C)
Huntington's chorea (PD) (L)	Treacher-Collins
	syndrome
Hypercholesterolaemia (PD) (L)	Tuberous sclerosis (E)
Marfan syndrome	von Hippel-Lindau
	disease (C)
Multiple endocrine neoplasia (C)	Waardenburg syndrome
	Wilm's tumour (C)

Table 2.5. *Continued*

Autosomal recessive

Bloom syndrome (PD) (C) (L)
Congenital adrenal hypoplasia (T) (PD)
Cystic fibrosis (PD) (L)
Cystinuria (T)
Friedrich's ataxia (L)
Galactosaemia (PD) (T)
Gauchier disease (PD)

Hepatolenticular
  degeneration (T)
Phenylketonuria (PD) (T)
Tay–Sachs disease (PD) (L)
Thalassaemia, alpha and
  beta (PD) (L) (T)
Xeroderma pigmentosum
  (C) (PD)

Multifactorial conditions

Condition	Genetic defect	Environmental factor
Sudden severe haemolytic anaemia	X-linked gene for G6PD	Some drugs, mothballs, some beans (including *Vicia fava* — hence 'favism')
Acute intermittent porphyria (abdominal pain, vomiting, respiratory paralysis)	Autosomal dominant gene for the enzyme uroporphyrinogen synthetase	Some drugs, infections, starvation
Sensitivity to succinylcholine (muscle paralysis and difficult breathing)	Gene for serum cholinesterase	Succinylcholine often used in surgical operations
Malignant hyperpyrexia (very high temperature, extreme tension, death)	Autosomal dominant gene	General anaesthetic

(C) = Cancer a likely complication; (E) = epilepsy a likely complication; (F) = fertility affected; (L) = early lethality; (PD) = prenatally diagnosable; (T) = treatment ameliorates condition.

normal at birth but at around 6–8 months of age they progressively develop kidney stones and severe gout, and involuntary movements which become worse, with 'eating' of lips and fingers, and profound mental retardation), some haemophilias and a variety of ichthyosis (hardening of the skin). Sons inherit defective X-chromosomes only from their mothers, but daughters from either parent (Fig. 2.13). X-linked recessive conditions are expressed only in males, for in females the abnormal X would be 'inactivated' in about *half* of all the cells (inactivation occurs randomly between maternal and paternal X-chromosomes), leaving the normal X to compensate throughout the body for the ill-effect of the gene on the active Xs. Accordingly, if a woman has a brother or maternal uncle who suffered from, say, Duchenne muscular dystrophy, she could well be a 'carrier' (i.e. have the gene but

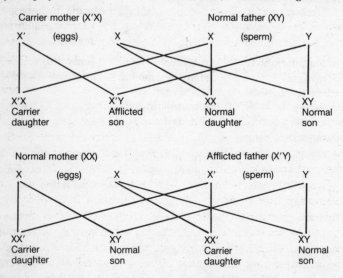

Fig. 2.13 Normal women are XX in terms of their sex chromosomes, and normal men XY. Where the X-chromosome carries a faulty gene, it is identified as X′. It can be seen from this diagram that X-linked recessive conditions are expressed only in males; females have a normal X to compensate, and so are only 'carriers'.

show no symptoms) and this state can generally be recognized by blood analysis to detect the presence of what would be much larger concentrations than normal of a particular enzyme (creatine phosphokinase). If a pregnant woman is found to be a carrier, there would be a 50:50 chance that her fetus, if male, would develop the disease.

Of particular interest, for the reason that they could be the most amenable to treatment by the technique of genetic engineering, specifically by means of gene transfer, are the disabilities classed as single-gene disorders (including the X-linked anomalies just dealt with). More than 3000 such genes are known, and about 1000 have been defined in detail and cloned; most are very rare but in total the group could account for defects in about 1 per cent of the whole human population. Some are classed as 'autosomal dominants', which means that the defective genes are carried by chromosomes other than the sex chromosomes. Among the more familiar conditions caused are the following: *Achondroplasia†*— the typical circus dwarf; although mentally bright and generally healthy, they do suffer from back problems. *Huntington's chorea (disease)*—symptoms begin commonly in the 40s, with irregular uncontrollable movements, progressive mental deterioration, and early death. *Neurofibromatosis†*—curvature of the spine, some mental defect, sometimes seizures, and on the body surface many brown patches ('*café-au-lait* spots') and non-malignant growths.

Then there are the 'autosomal recessives', which include the following: *Cystic fibrosis*—the most common birth defect in western countries, affecting about 1:1600 births. It is characterized by the formation of blockages in the various ducts and passages in the body, resulting in general disturbed function; the children are constantly ill and generally die before reaching adulthood. *Tay–Sachs disease*—most common in Ashkenazi Jews, affecting 1:3600 births, but other people too. It involves progressive mental and physical degeneration

†About 80 per cent of cases of achondroplasia and 25 per cent of cases of neurofibromatosis are 'new mutations'[52] — no warning from family history!

until death occurs, generally by the age of 4 years. *Sickle-cell
disease*—affects the blood in such a way as to cause the red
cells to adopt strange sickle-like shapes (Fig. 2.14); they are
unable to carry oxygen efficiently, and tend to get impacted
in small blood vessels, causing blockages and hence much
trouble. In addition, severe chronic anaemia becomes evident
in infancy, from when there are bouts of fever and the feeling
of intense pain in bones and abdomen; many die in early
childhood, though survival can be increased by blood transfusions. The disease is most common in African and Mediterranean races. The *thalassaemias*, alpha and beta, affect very
large numbers of people around the world, particularly those
indigenous to the Mediterranean region. These are disorders
of haemoglobin production, of varying severity depending

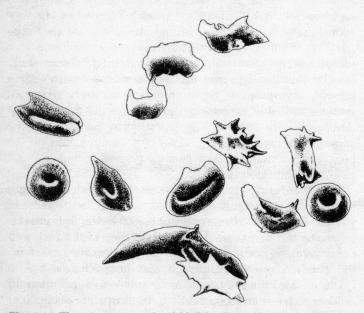

Fig. 2.14 The appearance of red blood cells in a case of 'sickle-cell'
anaemia; two normal cells are present, shaped like doughnuts.
(Drawn from several sources.)

on the number of faulty genes involved, the more serious forms usually being fatal.

In other conditions, environmental factors have a precipitating effect; examples include: *G6PD deficiency*—due to lack of an enzyme already mentioned, as specified by an X-linked gene, which may not be important unless certain drugs are taken or certain beans are eaten, when severe anaemia may develop. Other conditions are caused by interaction between several defective genes; examples are rheumatoid arthritis, epilepsy, and schizophrenia. Some defects can be picked up by appropriate tests before birth, such as *spina bifida*, which, with other spinal and brain defects, occurs in about 16 of every 1000 conceptions, about half of which are aborted. In spina bifida, the vertebral column is incomplete in the back, allowing the spinal cord to protrude, sometimes still covered by skin but in other cases exposed. There is paralysis of the legs and lack of control over emptying of bladder and rectum. The children usually die within a year unless they get surgical treatment, but this still leaves them paraplegic. Exposure of the spinal cord in spina bifida and related defects releases fluids containing a fetal serum protein, alphafetoprotein, which passes into the amniotic cavity and can be detected by amniocentesis.

Prevention, early diagnosis, and treatment

So much success has been achieved in dealing with diseases caused by viruses, moulds, bacteria, and protozoa (sometimes amounting to eradication) that there is mounting pressure to do the same with genetic diseases.

Prevention generally depends on the establishment of a 'preventive genetic register' based on careful analyses of family histories as ascertained by interviews and questionnaires. From such a compilation, the prospects of families at risk can be assessed and decisions made by the parents whether to take a chance on initiating a pregnancy or be prepared to accept elective abortion, in the event of evidence being obtained of anomalous embryonic or fetal development. Alternatively, the couple might prefer artificial insemination with donor's semen, or adoption, or even consider the possibilities of a surrogate arrangement (discussed in Chapter 4), depending on whether it is the husband or wife that carries the defective gene. On the other hand, if the risk involves the transmission of an X-linked gene, the husband's semen may be treated for the removal of sperm carrying the Y-chromosome (thus preventing or rendering unlikely the birth of males, who, as explained in the previous section, alone express X-linked recessive traits). It should be stressed that the separation of X- and Y-bearing sperm in the laboratory is not yet a fully reliable procedure, but the experiences of some investigators look highly promising.[97,98] Finally, there are indications that the frequency with which neural tube defects like spina bifida recur in families can be reduced by giving the mother an improved diet, especially with additional vitamin intake.

Analysis of eggs or embryos before the stage of implantation, and the decision not to transfer those found to be carrying genetic defects, thus avoiding the actual establishment of a pregnancy, could be regarded as possible methods for 'prevention', but it seemed more appropriate to deal with them in the next section.

Early diagnosis can be a great help in the management of genetic disease. Ideally, evidence for genetic problems should be detectable at the *gamete* stage, and indeed some progress has been made here. Some years ago, Ryuzu Yanagimachi and his colleagues introduced the 'hamster egg penetration test' (see Chapter 3, p. 91) for assessing the fertilizing potential of human sperm,[39] and this turned out to have a very important spin-off; if fertilization was allowed to proceed, the sperm chromosomes came to be displayed in the egg cytoplasm (as normally happens in the final stage of fertilization, just before egg and sperm chromosome groups unite in syngamy).[99-101] This permits an examination of chromosome number and structure, such things as inver-

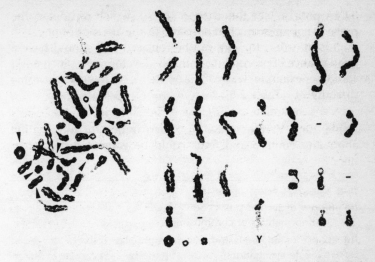

Fig. 2.15 Human sperm chromosomes as they come to be displayed in the egg cytoplasm, in the 'hamster egg penetration test' (left); the method can clearly show the presence of abnormal chromosomes (marked by arrow heads). On the right, chromosomes are arranged in systematic order, revealing that several are abnormal, three are missing, and there are three anomalous fragments. There would be little chance that such a patient (who was, in fact, receiving radiotherapy for cancer) could father normal children. (From ref. 101.)

sions, translocations, deletions, and duplications (see pp. 62–4) being diagnosable (Fig. 2.15).† Similar information could be obtained for human eggs, if sufficient numbers can be obtained to be used in this way, and thus examination of both gametes could be invaluable for assessing the risks inherent in a planned pregnancy. The female gamete can also be investigated in another way—when the second polar body is extruded in response to sperm penetration (Chapter 1, p. 7), the chromosomes in it can be tested by the technique of

†If the Infertility (Medical Procedures) (Amendment) Act 1984 (see Chapter 5, p. 126) becomes law in Victoria, Australia, this is the kind of information that would become available. [This Act became law in 1988.]

'DNA probes' (see this chapter, p. 59), which can detect the presence of an extra chromosome, or the absence of one;[11,82] if all is in order, the egg can be replaced and should have a good chance of proceeding with full development. Such a test could, for example, warn of the existence of Down's syndrome (trisomy-21) (Table 2.6).

Table 2.6. Various ways in which important information about the embryo and fetus could be gained during pregnancy

---

First 3 months of pregnancy
(a) Biopsy of second polar body
    Abnormalities of chromosomes

(b) Biopsy of single blastomeres or trophoblast cells
    Sex determination
    Chromosomes anomalies
    Assay of some enzymes (HPRT, G6PD)
    Analysis of DNA (cystic fibrosis, haemophilia, etc.)

(c) Biopsy of chorionic villi (prolonged culture usually not necessary)
    Sex determination
    Chromosome anomalies
    Detection of inborn errors of metabolism
    DNA analysis (Huntington's disease, cystic fibrosis, etc.)

Second 3 months of pregnancy and later
(d) Amniocentesis (culture of cells usually necessary)
    Sex determination
    Chromosome anomalies
    Detection of inborn errors of metabolism
    Detection of alpha-fetoprotein
    DNA analysis

(e) Ultrasonography (a completely safe procedure)
    As an aid to chorionic villus biopsy and amniocentesis.
    Detection of spina bifida, anencephaly (failure of brain to develop), severe limb defects and dwarfing, congenital heart disease.

(f) Radiography
>   Helps in the detection of skeletal abnormalities — best at 20
>   weeks, but rarely used nowadays.

(g) Nuclear magnetic resonance (NMR) imaging
>   An alternative to ultrasonography, completely safe and
>   giving a better image of both soft and hard tissues, but not
>   yet widely available.

(h) Fetoscopy
>   An endoscope (a very thin fibre-optic telescope) is passed
>   through the walls of the abdomen and uterus; it allows
>   direct observation of parts of the fetus, and also aids getting
>   blood samples as well as biopsy specimens of internal
>   organs, etc.

Possibilities become more numerous with cleavage embryos. Investigations on the embryos of laboratory and agricultural animals have shown that single blastomeres can be taken from 2- and 4-cell stages, and small numbers of cells from the trophectoderm of blastocysts, without seriously jeopardizing the embryo's prospects for full development (as mentioned on pp. 40, 60). In mice with a murine equivalent of the Lesch–Nyhan syndrome (the human form is briefly described on pp. 66, 68), analysis of cell samples permitted identification of affected male embryos and carrier females. The embryos were returned to the uterus and the affected genetic status confirmed later at the advanced fetal stage. Some of the conceptuses were allowed to continue and live young were born.[102,103] For the human subject, these points are relevant, not only for embryos grown in the laboratory after fertilization *in vitro*, but also for those flushed from the uterus after a normal initiation of pregnancy, preparatory to transfer as a donated embryo or return to its mother after due inspection. The manipulations of recovery from and return to the uterus impose no greater interference for the woman than she would experience in, say, the fitting of an IUD. Blastocysts treated in this way have been found to undergo implantation and give rise to normal term infants,[104] and could serve as sources of cells for analysis, as with the mouse material just mentioned, but this procedure is at present essentially precluded with human embryos.

Less problematic now could be exploitation of the 'non-invasive' approach, in which embryos (human as well as mouse) are held in small volumes of culture medium for about 24 hours, and the medium is then analysed by highly refined techniques to measure the uptake of various nutrients, the release of waste products, enzymes, and hormones, and the production of special items like the 'early pregnancy factor' (noted in Chapter 1, pp. 10, 13) and the 'platelet activating factor'.[105] This approach, still in its infancy, is certainly full of promise. (Whether analysis is made on samples of the embryos themselves or on samples of culture medium, it is important to keep in mind that gene expression in the human embryo begins between the 4- and 8-cell stages—before that, it is the maternal genome that is being expressed in the cells of the embryo.)[106]

By contrast, methods that can be applied to the examination of postimplantation embryos and of fetuses have received much more attention, and now represent a valuable battery of well-tried techniques. They include biopsy of chorionic villi, amniocentesis, ultrasonography, radiography, NMR (or MR) imaging and fetoscopy (Table 2.6).[11,52,53,107-9]

Biopsy of chorionic villi, which derived from the fertilized egg and are part of the placenta (Fig. 1.7) and therefore have the same genetic constitution as the fetus, is not a difficult task when performed at 8–12 weeks of pregnancy (Fig. 2.16)[110] A special advantage is that the tissues in this region at this time are multiplying particularly rapidly, so that sufficient cells for analysis may be available immediately or can be obtained after a short period of culture. A somewhat worrying note, though, has been struck by some investigators who have reported a degree of 'mosaicism' (variability) in chromosome number in samples of villus tissue; clearly, this will need to be watched with some care. Greater versatility in the diagnosis of anomalies is provided by material obtained by amniocentesis (Fig. 2.17),[111] which can be performed at

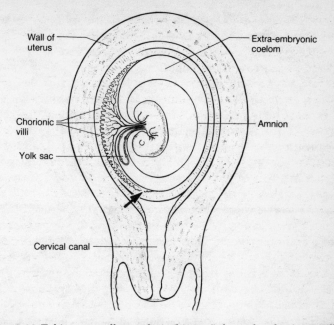

Fig. 2.16 Taking a small sample (a 'biopsy') from the chorionic villi (illustrated also in Fig. 1.7) is possible with an instrument passed up through the cervical canal to the point indicated by the large arrow, or else by means of a long hypodermic needle inserted through the abdominal wall.

around 16–18 weeks of pregnancy; fetal cells floating in the amniotic fluid can be cultured and studied, but some delay is incurred because cleavage rates are relatively slow and it takes time to get enough cells. Both methods are assisted by ultrasonography (ultrasound scanning). The amniotic fluid can be tested for the presence of alphafetoprotein (mentioned on p. 71 as associated with neural tube defects, including not only spina bifida but also hydrocephalus—swelling of the brain and skull caused by pressure in the fluid within), and a biochemical test is also possible (estimating the amount of the enzyme acetylcholinesterase). Both chorionic villus biopsy

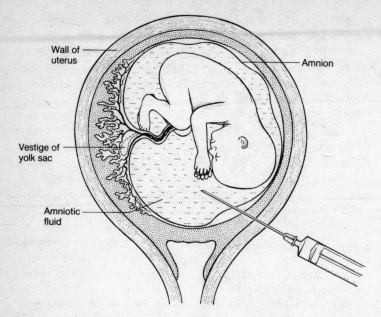

Fig. 2.17 Amniocentesis—the sampling of amniotic fluid by means of a hypodermic needle and syringe.

and amniocentesis involve risks of inducing abortion, but probably not to the extent of more than one in 200 pregnancies.

Fetoscopy requires the insertion of a very fine fibre-optic telescope into the amniotic cavity, so that the fetus itself can be surveyed for identification of sex and for anatomical defects, and to assist in other procedures, such as the taking of blood or tissue samples from the fetus. Ultrasonography can be used to detect major anatomical defects in the fetus (even some heart defects), and has the advantage of being easy to apply and completely safe for mother and child. The fetus casts a detectable shadow by radiography as early as 10 weeks, but the best time for examination by this method is 20 weeks, when skeletal defects can be recognized; the procedure is rarely used nowadays. Nuclear magnetic resonance

(NMR) imaging gives a much better picture than ultrasonography and also has no deleterious effect on the subject; if the costs can be reduced by the use of permanent magnets, this is likely to be the method of choice.[107]

Treatment of human embryos and fetuses is at present very limited in scope, though there are possibilities that could be realized in a few years time (see pp. 57, 82). If there is evidence that a rhesus negative (Rh−) mother is damaging the fetus by the production of antibodies against the fetal red blood cells (in the condition known as 'haemolytic disease of the newborn'), the fetus can be given a blood transfusion with the aid of fetoscopy. Hydrocephalus in the fetus (an excess of fluid in the brain, due generally to blockage in the normal exit for the fluid) can be treated surgically, increasing the chances of normal birth as well as improving the recovery prospects of the fetus. Some disturbances in the metabolism (turnover of nutritive materials) in the fetus can be ameliorated by appropriate diets for the mother.

On the other hand, treatment after birth has considerable potential, much aided by prenatal diagnosis which facilitates an early start. Children born with phenylketonuria (a disturbance of metabolism), for example, have much better prospects with early treatment, which consists simply of a special diet with a low content of the amino acid phenylalanine. If treatment is delayed, the children can suffer mental retardation. The serious anaemia known as beta thalassaemia is often fatal soon after birth, unless the child receives regular blood transfusions. Haemophilia, 'bleeders disease', can be kept at bay by treatment with the particular blood-coagulation factor that is missing. Administration of sex hormones can often correct the symptoms of conditions due to anomalies of the sex chromosomes. Similarly, appropriate hormone treatment can alleviate the symptoms of congenital adrenal hyperplasia, which in baby girls often shows as abnormal development of the vulva and clitoris, but can become a serious condition in both sexes without treatment. Even anomalies due to several aberrant genes acting together, the so-called 'multifactorial disorders', can be improved greatly by corrective surgery or suitable medication. Among these conditions is an old acquaintance, namely diabetes mellitus, which was first successfully treated with insulin in 1922.

A procedure that has become much more effectively used in recent years is bone marrow transplantation. It has been found especially valuable for treating 'severe combined immunodeficiency' or SCID (the 'boy in the bubble' syndrome), beta thalassaemia, and other genetically determined blood disorders, as well as anaemia due to other causes, and leukaemia. In many instances, treatment has led to long-term survival, equivalent to 'cure'.[112,113] An additional manoeuvre is to treat the bone marrow outside the body by means of recombinant DNA technology and then return it if tests show that the introduced genes are normally functional (see pp. 58–9).

A few years ago, a novel method of treatment was introduced by Mexican doctors who transplanted parts of the brain and the adrenal glands from an aborted fetus into the brains of two people suffering from Parkinson's disease[114,115]—a condition thought to be attributable to a deficiency of the substance 'dopamine', which functions in the brain in the transmission of impulses from one nerve cell to another—with the aim of increasing the production of dopamine. The trial has worked satisfactorily so far, both patients showing dramatic improvement. Though there is still a possibility of graft rejection, fetal tissue seems likely to have low antigenicity, and experience elsewhere suggests that the brain may be a 'privileged site' and unlikely to develop an immune reaction.[116] Parkinson's disease is not certain to have a major genetic component, but the case illustrates the possible value of fetal tissue for transplantation and could provide a less hazardous procedure than gene transfer. More recently, fetal brain tissue transfer has been carried out in other centres, not only for Parkinson's disease but also as a treatment for Huntington's disease, which is attributable to a faulty gene (see pp. 66, 69), and for

Alzheimer's disease, another degenerative condition associated with ageing but with no known immediate cause.[117]

What might be gained by further experiments on human embryos?

The present state of the technology that makes it possible for IVF+ET to be performed at success rates of 10–20 per cent (in the longer-established and more experienced clinics)[118] was achieved only through experimentation. Tests with the embryos of laboratory animals had established the essential procedures, but there was, and still is, much room for improvement. In the newer clinics, success rates are often well below 10 per cent, and may even be around 1–2 per cent, in terms of babies born per treatment session,[119] and improvement must depend upon 'trying out' ideas culled from the literature, or learned about at scientific meetings, or gained through personal contacts in the more successful clinics—all this of course means experimentation. Even under the best conditions that can at present be defined, however, embryos cultured in the laboratory do not develop as rapidly or as surely as those remaining in the mother's body,[120] and it is important from all points of view that further technical improvements be made. A detail often overlooked, for example, is the purity of the water used for making up the culture medium—it may contain deleterious organic substances or metallic ions, and require especially rigorous methods of purification.[121,122] Even minute traces of some detergents clinging to glassware or instruments can have drastic effects on cells in culture. Testing with animal embryos can provide valuable indications, but involvement finally of the human embryo is essential, owing to differing susceptibilities.

The situation is much the same with the various forms of manipulation. Cryopreservation, for example, still represents a bigger risk for human embryos than for cattle embryos, because so much more has been done by way of experiment to find the optimal conditions for cattle embryos; the effects of

several variables in freezing procedures used for human
embryos have recently been reported.[123] Then there are
methods like the removal and analysis of the second polar
body from the egg before fertilization, which could provide
information on the genetic health of the prospective
embryo.[11] Similarly with the 'sampling' of early embryos,
involving the removal of a blastomere from a 4- or 8-cell
embryo or a few cells from a blastocyst, or even the 'halving'
of a morula or blastocyst, procedures which have been shown
in laboratory and agricultural animals to be well tolerated and
could help to avoid establishment of an anomalous conceptus. Application of these and related new procedures in
human medicine inevitably involves experimentation, but
they could be of great help in assuring prospective parents of
the birth of a healthy child.

More distant possible gains from experimentation on
human embryos relate to procedures at present still firmly
limited to non-human subjects, and include the use of
'embryonic stem cells' (ES cells) derived from blastocysts, cell
lines from postimplantation embryos, and the applications of
genetic engineering (or recombinant DNA technology, see
pp. 50–60). Work with mice and hamsters has shown that ES
cells can be obtained by culturing blastocysts under special
conditions, when these cells grow out and can be collected for
separate culture. The unique feature of ES cells is that they
can be grown in the laboratory for (it seems) an indefinite
period and yet retain a normal behaviour and chromosome
number; in addition, they can be described as 'pluripotential',
which means that they can develop, if introduced into an
embryo, into any kind of body cell (Fig. 2.18).[124–6] The
mechanism of many genetic diseases involves the abnormal
production, or no production at all, of a hormone or other
agent required by many tissues for their normal metabolism,
and in consequence normal functions fail to materialize, but if
healthy cells of the appropriate genetic constitution are introduced into the body, they can repair the deficiency by differ-
entiating into tissues that provide the wanted item. Support

Fig. 2.18 A chimeric mouse that developed from a white mouse's blastocyst, into which embryonic stem cells (ES cells) from a pigmented strain were injected. (Based on data in ref. 126.)

for the idea comes from observations, mostly in mice, on experimental chimeras formed between cleavage embryos: deficiencies in one component are completely compensated for ('rescued') by the normal component (see this chapter, pp. 41–3). One example of this is the rescue of a parthenogenetic embryo following fusion with a normal embryo, as described on pp. 44, 45. Another relates to mouse embryos carrying a faulty gene responsible for a condition known as 'testicular feminization'; in this, all males are infertile because their testes fail to produce any sperms. But if a male embryo with this gene is made to form a chimera with a normal male embryo, the product grows up to be a normal male mouse, with cells carrying the defective gene actually sharing in the process of fertile sperm production.

The process of chimera formation between two embryos

seems at present to have little potential value in human medicine, but chimerism produced by the incorporation of ES and other cell lines into embryos, fetuses, and human subjects after birth surely does have such value, especially if the cell lines carry selected genes, possibly inserted by means of genetic engineering (see pp. 58–9).[81,127] The same kind of approach is seen in work on the injection of specific tissue lines into animals after birth. Stem cells of the variety that will develop into blood-cell-forming tisue (haemopoietic cell lines) have been obtained from 6–7-day mouse embryos and injected into young or adult animals that were genetically defective or had been treated with X-rays to destroy their haemopoietic tissue; normal red blood cell production was restored.[128] There are also, in theory, prospects of culturing precursor cells for various tissues and organs from late human embryos or early fetuses, with the object of transferring these cells later to patients urgently needing transplants from sources that would not provoke rejection through an immune reaction.[129] Major ethical problems attach, of course, to the culture of embryos and fetuses specifically for this purpose.[115]

An idea that has often been mooted is that differentiated tissues and even organs from (aborted) fetuses might be cultured in the laboratory and, if necessary, also 'banked' in low-temperature storage for future transplantation to patients in need, much as with the blood and semen banks of today. But there are major difficulties. Cells from differentiated tissues generally do not grow well in culture for long— after a while they undergo a change known as 'malignant transformation', becoming in fact cancer cells, and then they grow extremely well! During their period of normal growth, they can be cryopreserved, just as sperm can, but are likely to exist only in small numbers at that time. With the qualifications just made, cells culture well while they are individuals —when they compose larger structures like late embryos and fetuses, the problems multiply, mainly because of the relative inaccessibility of the inside cells to oxygen and nutrients and for the release of carbon dioxide and other wastes. Similarly with cryopreservation, which technically means storage at $-196\,°C$; as the outside tissues freeze, salts migrate to the inner unfrozen regions and soon reach concentrations that 'pickle' the tissues there.

3

The reasons for infertility

Infertility in a couple (not attributable simply to a policy of childlessness) may be defined as 'the inability of the man to impregnate or of the woman to conceive, owing to causes that may turn out to be correctable'. Then the intractable or 'hopeless' cases should be labelled 'sterile', although the usual medical interpretation of this term is the inability to *produce* sperm or eggs.

There are many causes of infertility and these could be classed as anatomical, physiological, or psychological; or as congenital (existing from birth) or acquired; or as due to diet, climate, or other environmental factors, including bacteria, protozoa, or viruses. The simplest approach is to consider the commonest causes.

Why are women infertile?

Most often it is because they have 'pelvic inflammatory disease' (PID), which about 2 per cent of adolescents develop each year. About 15 per cent of women become infertile after a single infection. The causative organisms are bacteria (usually *Neisseria gonorrhoeae*, *Mycoplasma hominis*, and *Chlamidia trachomatis*), and in 50–75 per cent of cases these are transmitted by sexual intercourse. But there are many other causes, and other organisms responsible include common ones not usually associated with disease, such as the ubiquitous *Escherichia coli*, a normal inhabitant of the intestines. PID is a serious condition, sometimes initiated by the wearing of an intrauterine device (IUD), or by the medical procedures of vacuum aspiration (insertion of a tube into the uterus to withdraw fluid) or hysterosalpingography (see Fig. 3.1), or by the check-up performance of 'dilatation and curettage' (D & C)

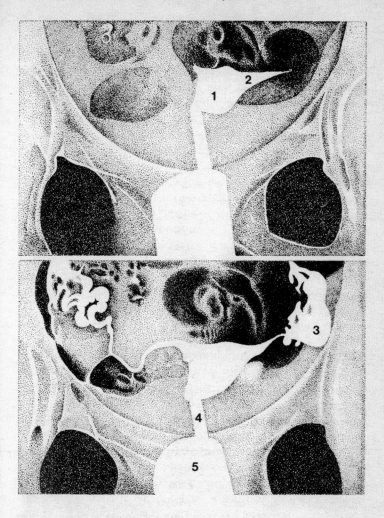

Fig. 3.1 Hysterosalpingography—the lower abdomen examined by means of X-rays. A test solution, opaque to X-rays, is injected into the uterus (1), from where it can be seen to flow through an oviduct (2) and into the abdominal cavity (3). The test finally showed that both oviducts were open. Shadows marked 4 and 5 were cast by the instruments used to make the injection. (From ref. 130.)

The reasons for infertility

done to detect early signs of uterine cancer (cervical carcinoma). Sometimes PID follows an attack of appendicitis or peritonitis, owing to spread of the infection, or even to a previous pregnancy or an abortion. Whatever the origin, the responsible organisms pass along the female tract, affecting the vagina and uterus little but causing injury to the oviducts and, after entering the abdominal cavity, damaging also the ovary. Infected oviducts become intensely inflamed, and in consequence are subject to the formation of much scar tissue ('fibrosis' and 'adhesions'), which often leads to complete closure of the tube, so that not even the minute sperm can get through, and also distortion which makes any sort of surgical repair difficult or even impossible. The specialized opening of the oviduct (the 'infundibulum'), with its fringe ('fimbria') of delicate finger-like projections (Figs 1.2 and 1.5), are particularly vulnerable to damage by infection, so that the normal function of these structures—the 'pick-up' of the eggs from the follicles—is no longer possible. The surface layers of the ovary also become greatly thickened, so that the follicles in which the eggs develop cannot open to release them.

When an infertile couple requests help that might take the form of the test-tube baby procedure, one of the first moves is to make an examination by means of a laparoscope (a description of which was given in Chapter 2, pp. 34, 35), which enables the surgeon to inspect the oviduct and ovary, and he can soon decide whether the infertility is likely to be due to the infection. Not only must he determine whether or not the oviduct is completely obstructed (tested by hysterosalpingography), but also whether there is a prospect of the ovarian follicles opening to release eggs, i.e. whether ovulation can occur. Sometimes the ovary surface has become so thickened and covered with adhesions that even after the surgeon has removed the offending tissue with 'cautery' the eggs cannot escape or be extracted from the ovary. More commonly, it is only the oviduct that is occluded, and the eggs can be extracted from the follicles for fertilization in the laboratory.

Quite often, severe damage is restricted to the ovarian end of the oviduct, the rest of the organ retaining reasonably normal function; a procedure known as GIFT (discussed in Chapter 4, pp. 94, 96) can then be used, in which sperm and eggs are put together for fertilization in the more uterine regions of the oviduct.

Infertility can also be caused by 'endometriosis', a strange condition in which cells from the lining of the uterus become displaced, pass through the oviducts and take up residence in the abdominal cavity on the surface of various organs there, including the oviducts and ovaries. During menstruation, these groups of cells go through the same changes as the normal cells in the uterus, and for some reason this causes pain. In addition, the condition is associated with disturbance to normal reproductive function.

A serious but less common reason for infertility is a condition known as 'primary amenorrhoea', in which menstrual cycles fail to start at puberty and no extraneous cause can be identified. It is attributable to a basic endocrine inadequacy which can be overcome sometimes by appropriate hormone injections. One of the early test-tube baby successes achieved by the Australian team led by Carl Wood and Alan Trounson was in a woman with primary amenorrhoea; it was necessary to compensate for the condition by suitable hormone treatment before *and throughout* the pregnancy.[131] Much more common is 'secondary amenorrhoea', the lack of menstrual cycles brought on by undernutrition or frank starvation (as in 'slimmers' disease' or 'anorexia nervosa'), or prolonged strenuous exercise, as seen in women athletes, dancing enthusiasts, and the like.[132]

'Polycystic ovaries' can certainly be an adequate reason for infertility. The term describes a condition in which the follicles bearing the eggs enlarge in the usual way but then go on to get bigger and bigger—just why, is not known for certain. The condition is associated with various hormone irregularities, which is why the affected women also suffer from lack of or unpredictable menstrual cycles, the growth of facial hair and obesity, and of course infertility. The disorder is also known as the 'Stein–Leventhal syndrome'.

The cells lining the female reproductive tract are capable of reacting to the presence of a foreign protein by producing antibodies against it; normally, the foreigners are bacteria, so this is just a defence against infection (by no means 100 per cent efficient, as we have seen!). Sometimes ('by mistake'), the reaction is mounted against sperm and can be sufficiently intense to prevent sperm from taking part in fertilization. The highest concentration of antibodies tends to be in the mucus in the cervical canal connecting the vagina and the uterus, and this is a conveniently obtainable material for testing in the laboratory for the presence of anti-sperm antibodies; if the test is positive, the mucus is said to be 'hostile', and hostile mucus accounts for quite a number of infertile cases.

Then again, women can be infertile because of psychological reactions against the idea of intercourse. As a result, there may be involuntary contractions of the wall of the vagina ('vaginismus') preventing full insertion of the penis. The problem can usually be overcome by psychotherapy.

Finally, in 5 to 10 per cent of cases of infertility—according to some reports, as many as 25 per cent—no adequate cause can be found, pointing up our need for much more information in this field.

Why are men infertile?

In nearly a third of infertile couples, the cause lies mainly or entirely with the man. Probably the commonest reason is the condition known as 'oligospermia', which simply means that the man has too few sperm in his semen for there to be realistic chances of sexual intercourse resulting in fertilization. It is indeed, to some extent, always a matter of *chance*, and so no-one can really give a figure for the minimum number of sperm necessary to achieve fertilization—as the numbers fall, the odds lengthen. Most recommendations, however, are for at least 5 million sperm in each millilitre of semen. And many men have fewer than this! If no sperm can be detected at all, the sample is described as 'azoospermic'. But number is not the only criterion—the sperm that are present in a sample acceptable as fertile must have good motility, i.e. have vigorously lashing tails and fast forward movement through the medium. In addition, only a very small minority of the sperm should show structural abnormalities, such as missing heads (they *can* swim without those!), deformed acrosomes, or twisted tails, but function tests should also be applied[133]—these include the 'hamster egg penetration test'.[39,134] In this test, hamster eggs freed from their zonas are placed in a suspension of human sperm, and incubated. Human sperm of normal fertility are able to become attached to the surface of these eggs and fuse with them; the sperm nuclei then move into the eggs and change into male pronuclei, just as though they had entered human eggs. If the sperm lack normal fertility, these events do not occur, and sperm infertility unexplained by sperm number, motility, or structure has often been revealed by means of this test.

Men are infertile for a number of other reasons also. Some, like the women we have just considered, are infected with the gonococcus and other disease organisms, others have suffered swelling of and damage to the testis ('orchitis') as a result of an attack of mumps, and others again are infertile because they have become immunized to their own sperm. Sometimes, the testes fail to 'descend' from the abdominal cavity, where they normally reside until a late stage of fetal development, and so do not take up their accustomed place in the scrotum, and as a result spermatogenesis is severely affected. This cause of male infertility is referred to as 'cryptorchidism' and should be recognized and corrected early in life (preferably before the age of 6 years) if the effect is to be overcome. The reason is that scrotal temperature is about 2.5 °C below that of the abdomen, and the lower temperature is essential for normal sperm production in human beings, as in most other mammals. Sometimes this feature of the scrotum is disturbed by the occurrence of 'varicocoele'—abnormal dilatation of blood vessels supplying the testis, resulting in increased blood flow into that region and hence increased local temperature.

There is a variety of other reasons for male infertility. During early fetal development, the sperm (and urinary) duct in the penis begins by being a deep groove and not a closed tube; closure to form a tube occurs normally at about the fourteenth week of pregnancy, but sometimes fails to do so by the time of birth, partially or completely. The result is the persistence of a slit along part or most of the length of the penis through which urine escapes and, at ejaculation, semen also; the condition is known as 'hypospadias'. Some men are unable to ejaculate normally because of structural peculiarities in the neck of the bladder, the semen passing into the bladder instead of along the urethra; others are unable to develop an erection, a condition termed 'impotence'. There are also dietary and occupational hazards that can cause infertility, including excessive consumption of alcohol, exposure to metals like lead, cadmium, and mercury, often encountered in heavy industry, various drugs and pesticides, chemicals used in cancer treatment, and, uniquely, the pigment 'gossypol' which is known to have sterilized many workers in the cottonseed oil industry in China. Male infertility can also accompany disorders of the sex chromosomes; men (normally XY) born with XXY ('Klinefelter's syndrome') or XX ('sex reversal') usually do not produce sperm; XYY males usually do.

4

Ways of overcoming the problem of infertility*

Infertile women—and test-tube babies—and surrogacy

The various procedures used for overcoming female infertility are set out in Table 4.1. Sometimes the problem is simplicity itself—one does nothing! It has become proverbial that a proportion of the women on the waiting list of any IVF+ET clinic will become pregnant before they see the doctor. In part, this is presumably due to relief of anxiety—at last, the nagging problem of childlessness will soon be in expert hands—and in part it is because with reduced fertility one has to keep trying for longer. So there are virtues in long waiting lists, but at this time counselling could be of particular help, and also as part of any treatment programme adopted.[135]

When the patient does eventually see the doctor, one of the first things for him to do is to determine whether she is in fact menopausal, which usually means that there are no eggs left in the ovary. If eggs are still there, are they being ovulated? This can conveniently be checked by estimating blood progesterone levels over a period—soon after ovulation in each cycle, progesterone rises to reach a peak about 5 days later. Then, a course of injections of progesterone can be given in order to induce growth of the uterine lining (the endometrium); when this is discontinued, there should be evidence of something like menstrual bleeding, and if this occurs the indications are that both ovary and uterus are functional. (Pregnancies have been established with hormonal treatment in women with non-functional ovaries[131] or no

*For a general review see ref. 137.

Table 4.1.   Methods for overcoming female infertility

Procedure	Salient features	References
Estes operation	Ovaries implanted in uterine walls, so that eggs ovulate into uterine cavity and are fertilized there by coitus or AI	W.L. Estes, born 1885
IVF+ET	Eggs from follicles, matured and fertilized *in vitro*, cultured for day or two, transferred to uterus	24, 129, 140
GIFT	Eggs from follicles, placed in oviducts with sperm	141
PROST	Eggs from follicles, fertilization begun *in vitro*, eggs into oviducts	142
TOT	As for GIFT, but with several special precautions	143
DIPI	Sperm injected into peritoneal cavity near oviduct openings	144
Egg or embryo donation	Donor eggs or embryos treated as for IVF+ET, GIFT, PROST, or TOT	
Surgery ± hormone treatment	Adhesions cut, oviduct reopened or rejoined, endometriosis removed	145,146
Hormone treatment	Ovulation failure attributable to hormone deficiency or imbalance	147
Administration of antibiotics	Infertility due to infections	148
Psychotherapy	Psychosexual problems	149,150
Surrogacy	Pregnancy physically impossible or unwanted	See pp. 99–101, 127–9

ovaries.)[136] Several other tests can be done, and if all results are satisfactory, the reason for the infertility must be sought elsewhere, and could take the form of infections or anomalies of the uterus and cervix, requiring appropriate treatment.[138,139]

Infections with the bacterium *N. gonorrhoeae* and other organisms can usually be dealt with effectively by treatment with penicillin derivatives. The extent of the damage caused by this infection can be assessed by laparoscopy, involving observation from within the abdominal cavity, or by hysterosalpingography (see Fig. 3.1), which involves the use of X-rays; if the oviducts are blocked, it is immediately evident by the latter method of examination. Oviduct obstruction and the commonly associated adhesions and tissue distortions can often be corrected adequately by surgical means. Whether normal function can be restored to the oviducts depends also on the degree of damage to the cells lining the insides of the tubes; these cells have numerous hair-like appendages (the cilia) which, by their vigorous waving motion, are responsible for the movement of the eggs from the ovarian end of the oviduct to the point where fertilization normally takes place. Other cells in this region produce secretions that are important in maintaining a healthy state within the oviduct and in providing an appropriate medium for the eggs and early embryos.

Surgical intervention commonly includes cutting through the major adhesions with a knife or by means of diathermy, and remaking the passageway through a blocked and shrunken oviduct by careful stretching and the dissection of smaller adhesions. One of the problems now is to prevent cut edges from growing together again, thus restoring the blockage; also, the act of cutting tissue inevitably causes some damage, with resultant contraction of the scar tissue. Sometimes a hopelessly blocked middle section of oviduct is cut out and the free ends joined up again. (Aspects of surgery and tubal repair are discussed in refs 151 and 152). A major risk of surgical correction in the oviduct is that repair may alter the function so that an 'ectopic' pregnancy occurs, when the embryo implants in the oviduct itself instead of in the uterus, or else, through abnormal function in the damaged tube, the embryo is passed back into the abdominal cavity and then implants on the surface of an organ there, commonly the ovary. Ectopic pregnancies are dangerous because they are so apt to cause haemorrhage, often serious enough to be fatal, and they may also lead to blockages of the alimentary tract; very rarely, ectopic pregnancies have been known to proceed into late pregnancy, when a viable child can be removed by Caesarian section. Owing to the risk to the mother's life, ectopic pregnancies are normally terminated without delay. In spite of these problems, surgical correction of damage done by infection can result in a rate of successful births as high as 10 per cent. Surgery may also be employed, together with hormone treatment, for the correction of 'endometriosis' (patches of uterus lining growing on the surfaces of abdominal organs, causing infertility), and here the subsequent birth rate can be as high as 50 per cent. (For further information, see refs 152–4.)

In some patients, in whom at least one of the oviducts has a modicum of normal function (originally or after corrective surgery), a procedure involving deposition of sperm and eggs into the oviduct has been employed successfully, fertilization taking place in the oviduct soon afterwards. This is known as the GIFT method (from gamete intrafallopian transfer, 'fallopian tube' being another name for oviduct), and a commendable rate of success has been claimed for it.[155–8] The procedure could also be used for patients with 'hostile cervical mucus', containing antibodies against sperm, specifically those of the sexual partner. Such a condition results in persistent infertility, which only sometimes responds to treatment with immunosuppressive drugs (which tend to prevent the production of antibodies). Success in such cases has also been reported to follow artificial insemination with a mixture of partner's and donor's semen.[159] Yet another way around the problem of hostile mucus is to inject a sperm suspension into the uterine cavity by means of a syringe with a long fine tube which is passed up through the vagina and cervix.[160] Finally, a sperm suspension could be injected into the abdominal cavity with the aid of a long hypodermic needle attached to the syringe, the sperm being deposited in the vicinity of the openings of the oviducts; this is known as *direct intraperitoneal insemina-tion* or DIPI. Sperm seem quite proficient at finding their way to and into the oviduct openings—as was first demonstrated in the rabbit as long ago as 1880.

If fertility cannot be restored by any of these means, recourse may be had to IVF+ET, the development of which was described earlier (Chapter 2, pp. 34–6).[25,140,161–6] Since its introduction, numerous improvements in method have been made. Ultrasound scanning to monitor both the har-vesting of the eggs from the ovary and the insertion of embryos in the uterus is much preferred to laparoscopy (and no doubt in due course NMR imaging—see Chapter 2, pp. 75, 76—will achieve pride of place); access to the abdomi-nal cavity through the wall of the vagina instead of the abdo-minal wall is considered to be an important surgical advance.[167] Quite recently, too, reports have described the passing of a thin tube (catheter) up through the vagina, cervix, and uterus, and thence into the oviduct, introducing sperm and eggs through this tube (or fertilized eggs, in the pro-nuclear stage or as 2-cell embryos)—this has been performed successfully on several occasions. Insertion of pronucleate eggs in the oviduct (by way of the uterus or through the abdominal opening of the tube) is referred to as PROST (from *pronuclear stage*),[168,169] and it has the important advantage that the patient need be in the clinic for a much shorter time, perhaps only hours, whereas for the procedure involving 2-cell embryos an extra day would likely be needed.

One of the main points of dissention among IVF clinics has to do with the number of eggs or embryos returned to the infertile woman, some clinics insisting on no more than *three*, others maintaining that better results are obtained with a larger number, and others again insisting that it is morally unacceptable *not* to return *all* the eggs and embryos. To some extent, the reasoning lies in the technical skills of the clinic, since the success rate must depend on refinement of methods; it depends partly on the procedure used—if normal fertilization and perhaps even cleavage can be *confirmed* before return of the eggs or embryos, this should assure better implantation rates—and partly on the fact that multiple pregnancies are a greater strain on the woman and are also increasingly liable to malfunction, and the larger the number of fetuses the shorter the pregnancy period, and so the less well prepared are the newborn for life 'outside'. This has led occasionally to the selective termination of implanted embryos in excess of three—widely regarded as ethically unacceptable.

Some couples feel strongly that the commonly used methods for overcoming female infertility not only offend moral and religious principles, but rob the act of generation of its important *personal* character—the bonds formed between a couple in the natural act of procreation can play a vital part in their relationship throughout marriage and parenthood. They maintain that IVF+ET and its variations are too 'mechanistic' and tend to conflict with a woman's intrinsic femininity. Some clinical aid is, of course, unavoidable, but would it not be possible (they ask) for things to be done in a more 'human' way? This point of view is surely very reasonable and has in fact received sympathetic consideration, a special procedure being developed in response.[143] Owing to the repugnance felt towards masturbation to obtain a semen sample, natural intercourse is used, the couple being instructed to indulge on two successive occasions about 6 hours apart, and on the second of these occasions, the man wears a *perforated* condom (with accordingly no contraceptive effect). Semen remaining in the condom is centrifuged and the sperm washed in the usual way. Eggs are obtained with the aid of laparoscopy after hormone treatment to promote follicle growth, and given a brief spell in culture during the collection period. The time between egg collection and their reintroduction into the patient is kept as short as possible (usually, it seems, only about 30 minutes) so that there is no opportunity for genetic assessment, or other manipulation. For the transfer, the eggs and sperm are drawn into a thin tube *separated* by an air space, and injected into an oviduct where fertilization takes place. Any eggs in excess of the recommended number are placed in the other oviduct, and the remaining sperm in the vagina. Such a method (referred to as TOT—*t*ubal *o*vum *t*ransfer) has yielded healthy births.

Of largely historic interest is the 'Estes operation' (named after W. J. Estes, born 1885), in which the ovaries of women with occluded oviducts were grafted into the wall of the uterus so that any eggs ovulated would pass into the uterine cavity and possibly be fertilized there—the scarcity of successes from this operation bears witness to the unreliability of the procedure. More recently, the transfer of oocytes directly to the uterus, with their later fertilization there following normal coitus, is similarly deficient in positive reports.

If treatment for infertility is unavailing and there are reasons to reject all the foregoing procedures, a further possibility lies in the arrangement constituting *surrogacy*, for which there is a significant demand despite its inherent legal difficulties (see Chapter 5, p. 127). The procedure depends on the making of an arrangement with another woman to carry a pregnancy to term on behalf of the patient. This system would appeal where a woman is infertile, indeed sterile, owing to lack or deficiency of the uterus, or because of removal of the uterus (hysterectomy) for various reasons, though she still possesses functional ovaries. There could be other reasons, too, such as a deep-seated psychological aversion to pregnancy, or simply unwillingness by someone like a professional model to prejudice her career by meeting the physical challenge of pregnancy. Commonly, surrogacy is undertaken for fee or reward, though sometimes for pure charity or for family reasons, as in a recent case where a mother in her forties acted as surrogate for an infertile daughter. The biology of the endeavour is simple enough, it is the moral, ethical and legal aspects that cause trouble. Some advocacy of the surrogate idea may be found in ref. 170.

The procedure may take one of four patterns:

(1) transfer to the surrogate's oviduct of the patient's eggs plus her husband's sperm, following the GIFT method just described;

(2) transfer to the surrogate of embryos recovered from the patient's oviduct after normal intercourse or the performance of an IVF procedure;

(3) if the patient cannot produce eggs, these may be obtained from a relative or a friend, fertilized *in vitro* by the husband's sperm, and the products transferred to the surrogate;

(4) if the patient cannot produce eggs, she may alternatively agree to the husband's sperm being used to fertilize the surrogate's eggs by artificial insemination.

If the husband cannot produce sperm, a donor's help may be enlisted in patterns (1) and (2). Legal problems associated with surrogacy are discussed briefly in Chapter 5, pp. 127–9, and see also ref. 171.

Another variation on the surrogacy theme took the form recently of a rather macabre suggestion in a daily paper that women who are declared 'brain-dead' as a result of an accident or other cause, but otherwise have a healthy body, and are being successfully maintained by life-support systems, could be impregnated and allowed to carry the pregnancies to term on behalf of infertile couples who were unable or unwilling to enter into the more usual arrangement. The notion would appear to be quite feasible, for the usual bodily functions in brain-dead people may continue until the support systems are switched off, and pregnancies can be carried to term with the hormonal status maintained artificially.[131] A brain-dead woman could presumably be treated as 'chattel', so the legal situation would be simplified, and from the ethical point of view, we are accustomed to the idea of the donation of organs for reuse when taken from the victims of accidents. But the general public reaction to the proposal was one of abhorrence, and the Church declared such an act as destructive of the dignity of the human person. Perhaps this could be regarded as an argument in favour of the development of methods of ectogenesis (discussed in Chapter 5, pp. 115–22).

Infertile men

Probably the commonest cause of male infertility lies in a deficiency of fertile sperm. This can often be improved by treatment for any bacterial or viral infections the man may be harbouring, correcting any gross dietary imbalances, reducing or eliminating smoking, or alcohol or other drug consumption, and ensuring that he wears clothing less likely to raise testis temperature by insulation. If these measures fail, improved chances of fertilization can sometimes be achieved by concentrating the sperms in the ejaculate by centrifugation, removing the overlying 'plasma' and resuspending the sperms in a good artificial diluent. If the sperm numbers in a subject's ejaculates are particularly low, several ejaculates can be pooled and the sperm concentratd by centrifugation. Further measures worth trying with sperm-poor ejaculates include injection of a resuspended preparation into the uterus, into the oviducts (perhaps along with eggs), or into the abdominal cavity. If all else fails, injection of individual sperms into eggs can be tried—this has been reported successful in a few experiments[172]—or the IVF+ET procedure adopted. If the husband's semen proves quite hopeless, the use of donor semen is an option; this course of action is also appropriate if the husband is known to be a carrier of a highly deleterious gene, especially if this is dominant.

In men who have developed an autoimmunity to their own sperm, the use of sperm recovered from the 'tail' of the epididymis (where it joins the vas deferens) (Fig. 1.3) is worth trying, as it is possible that the concentration of antibodies will be low or negligible there. Infections of the epididymis or the accessory glands (notably the prostate and seminal vesicles) can often be treated successfully with antibiotics. Although cryptorchidism, as a cause of infertility, should be treated early in life (as noted in Chapter 3, pp. 91, 92), there are instances on record in which surgical correction in adults was followed by fertile intercourse. Varicocoele (abnormal swelling of the veins of the testis) can also be corrected in adult life by surgery, which sometimes confers fertility. Vasectomy is a widely used method of male sterilization, and requests for reversal are not uncommon; 'recanalization' is frequently achieved but fertility not nearly so often restored. (Surgical treatment for infertility in men is discussed in ref. 173.)

5

Some aspects of ethics and law in assisted reproduction[15,19,174-6]

The danger of 'dehumanization'

In 1985, Senator Harradine introduced a Bill in the Australian Federal Parliament for a proposed 'Act to prohibit experiments involving the use of human embryos created by *in vitro* fertilization'. The Act referred specifically to preimplantation embryos and would permit experimentation but only if 'undertaken primarily for a benefit consistent with the development of the relevant human embryo's full human potential'. There were penal sanctions, namely a fine of $20 000 or imprisonment for 4 years. To determine the sense of public opinion about the proposed Act, a Senate Select Committee was appointed and held numerous meetings with representatives of all sections of the community; its full report occupies several volumes, but a manageable version is also available.[177] The Act itself is apparently not likely to materialize, for technical reasons, but the Bill certainly stimulated a considerable amount of debate. Popular reactions covered the full gamut from approval to disapproval, and revealed once again that many ordinary thinking people harbour an underlying distrust of the scientific community, suspecting it of planning or even performing many 'experiments' of an ethically dubious nature, especially in connection with human development. Ideas often centre about famous novels, such as Mary Shelley's *Frankenstein* and Aldous Huxley's *Brave New World* (some of these anxieties are discussed in this chapter: pp. 107–9), but this is a perennial feature of popular concern.

At the 1987 Annual Conference of the Australian and New Zealand Association for the Advancement of Science, Hiram

Caton delivered a well argued and pursuasive (and provoca-
tive) paper on the ethics of experimentation on human
embryos (his discussion also included other related activities,
such as selection and rejection of embryos on a genetic basis,
and elective abortion). He based this paper on the report of
the Senate Select Committee on the Harradine Bill, and found
abundant support there for the notion that doctors and scientists engaged in clinical work or research involving human
embryos are in the process of undergoing, or have already
undergone, 'dehumanization'.[178–180]

In Caton's view, such 'IVF scientists' 'make many state-
ments of an ethical nature' but do not 'undertake a systematic
defence of them, as ethicists do'. Hence, 'the ethical opinions
expressed by IVF scientists are fragmentary, undoctrinal, and
perhaps in some degree *ad hoc* or situation-dependent'. 'IVF
scientists seek to influence [regulatory] bodies to adopt
norms that permit what they perceive to be essential research
and clinical practice, but they accept that ethics procedures
may encumber research and practice'; 'the expressed ethical
views of IVF scientists comprise but a single dimension of
information; and when the normative formulae expressed in
that dimension are examined, it is apparent that indeed they
do not constitute ethics', but rather a set of 'effective values'.
In fact, the scientists themselves deny being ethicists. Nevertheless, by and large, scientists 'enjoyed an undisturbed good
conscience about IVF', and, faced with an ethically sensitive
situation, proceeded with their work 'weighing costs against
benefits on a sliding scale'—therapeutic gain against loss of
embryos; consistently, in medical practice there is acceptance
of the idea of 'non-therapeutic experimentation as integral
to contemporary medicine'. Research is considered to be
imperative if progress is to be achieved, and its direction
should not be subject to legal prohibitions. Some witnesses
before the Select Committee maintained that prohibition
would not in fact be effective, but would drive research
underground. On this, Caton comments: 'And there in the
twilight of illegitimacy scientists will concoct a terrible retri-

bution for those who would dare thwart research: they will create the very monster that terrifies moral feeling, the animal–human hybrid.'

From the foregoing characterization of the ethics of IVF scientists, a major source of motivation can be discerned as 'the therapeutic imperative', which derives from the interpretation of public support 'as a popular mandate for medical scientists to direct research wherever they may choose. Doubts that some research may lead up dangerous ethical, social, or economic paths are rebutted by exhibiting the distress alleviated by present remedies and anticipated breakthroughs'. And a mandate is assumed for scientists eventually to eliminate all defective genes from the human genome, but in the meantime to select embryos on the basis of genetic normality, discard the faulty and implant only the healthy, and, if a pregnancy is already established, to abort the fetuses found to be carrying genetic anomalies. These are of course eugenic procedures, but have so far been accepted with few qualms, despite the distant association with Nazi doctrine. And all of this, in Caton's view, stands in stark contrast to the time-honoured philosophy of traditional medicine, with its over-riding emphasis on human compassion and care. The welfare of the individual patient is lost in the absorption in biomedical technology and research; medicine has become a tool of social policy and now includes the administration of death— euthanasia for the terminally ill and elective abortion for the unwanted.

Undoubtedly, this line of argument embodies justifiable concern, and the reference to 'Nazi doctrine' is uncomfortably appropriate. The dream of a supreme Germanic race destined to dominate the Earth took powerful hold of the minds of many people in a great nation, before and during the early years of the 1939–45 World War. The systematic slaughter of 'inferior' human beings was an expression of that imagined superiority and provides persuasive evidence of flaws in human nature. As Francois de Menthon, a French representative at the Nuremberg Trials, said: 'The truly diabolical enterprise of Hitler and of his companions was to assemble in a body of dogmas formed around the concept of race all the instincts of barbarism, repressed by centuries of civilization, but always present in men's innermost nature'.[181]

What in fact did the Nuremberg Trials reveal that could be regarded as relevant to the ethics of doctors and scientists? As early as 1933, the German cabinet enacted 'The Law for the Prevention of Offspring with Hereditary Diseases', and medical economists provided mathematical support for this policy by calculating the high cost of maintaining the infirm. In *Mein Kampf*, Hitler states: 'The right of personal freedom recedes before the duty to preserve the race. There must be no half measures. It is a half measure to let incurably sick people steadily contaminate the remaining healthy ones'. So the system of euthanasia became established, initially to eliminate the incurable but very shortly extended to the undesirable, the carriers of 'inferior genes', and the 'useless eaters', which included the crippled, the aged, the insane, as well as foreign labourers no longer able to work. *And it is recorded that Hitler had no difficulty in finding doctors, nurses, and hospitals to obey all his orders.*

Justification for further extensions was found in the thinking that it was indefensible for German servicemen to be exposed to risks of injury and death, while unwanted 'inferior' people lived in relative safety in factories, farms, and concentration camps. Later, a similar argument was advanced in connection with the dangers that servicemen were exposed to in operating fighter aircraft, under conditions of intense cold and much reduced atmospheric pressure; experiments were clearly necessary to determine the limits of cold or low pressure that the body could stand. Unwanted people were used in huge numbers in these trials, with total disregard for their sufferings, and death was the regularly accepted 'end-point'. Callousness became completely ingrained and the brutal excesses never aroused comment among the observers, *nor in the nation as a whole*. And the sobering thought is that there is no guarantee that it will not all happen again.

Obviously, we must be on constant guard against the development of dehumanization, but to accept Caton's opinions wholeheartedly would surely mean the end of research-dependent progress in IVF work, genetic engineering, and the like. How we balance the pros and cons is very much a personal decision.[182]

In defence of the current approach by doctors and scientists to the problems of assisted reproduction, involving particularly embryo selection before transfer, and abortion of embryos and fetuses found to be defective, there are several points that can be made. These are relevant especially in the face of criticisms that embryo selection and disposal, and fetal testing and abortion, are simply 'the beginning'—that once these activities are socially and legally condoned, medical usage and popular acceptance of progressively more drastic procedures become inevitable. This notion is based on the 'slippery slope' argument, which states that there is an irresistible drive to more and more radical behaviour. As one newspaper commentator put it: 'Legalize abortion and you will soon have infanticide, and then, Nazi-style, the elimination of "inferior" people'. Once you are on the 'slope'—so the argument goes—sliding down is almost beyond control.

That line of argument is very frequently encountered, but is quite ill-founded. We have already been to the bottom of the 'slope' and in fact know the area well! A distressing feature of human history is the frequent recurrence of ruthless massacres—we know very well what it is to kill men, women, and children in large numbers, very often for purely doctrinal reasons. And when it comes to infanticide, this really is 'old hat'. The *Encyclopaedia Britannica* tells us that infanticide was a widely employed and time-honoured solution to various personal or social difficulties, and indeed continues to play this role in many places. Plato, it appears, actually recommended the killing of defective children in his *Republic*, and throughout history various people have found it expedient to destroy the newborn for what were, to them, adequate reasons—among the Eskimo, female newborn were killed because there might not be sufficient husbands to take care of them (critical in that harsh environment); in Polynesia, infanticide seemed necessary to avoid having the already dense population go too high; in the Hawaiian Islands, children beyond the third or fourth were disposed of with the same thought in mind; in Tahiti, chiefs had to kill their daughters (for presumably a more esoteric reason); in China, females were again the main victims or were sold as servants; in Africa, abnormal behaviour of the fetus or unusual birth presentations were sufficient justification for infanticide; in very many societies, and in some even to this day, extra-marital children were especially likely to be eliminated; in some areas, twins, triplets, etc. were routinely despatched as bearers of ill-omen; and finally, the first-born were often the preferred objects for religious offering (*Genesis* xxii), a practice that existed also in Egypt, Greece, Rome, and India.

Despite this dismal background, there are reasons to believe that human society (including the community of doctors and scientists), though liable by nature to occasional serious lapses, is becoming progressively more capable of maintaining a firm foothold on the slippery slope. In recent years, the evident social trend has been towards *increasing* concern for common-interest and ethical issues such as countryside preservation, the saving of endangered species, animal rights in general, and sundry human claims for special attention, such as international aid for famine relief. These movements testify to a burgeoning sensitivity for human values throughout the community, and an ever-widening determination to achieve higher levels in what we regard as the more commendable features of civilization.

Scientific medicine has the same ideals and goals. The work of the World Health Organization, together with numerous national and private bodies of similar intent, has done much to control and even eradicate diseases, and raise nutritional and general health standards in needy countries throughout the world. Of particular interest in the present context is the development and distribution of many contraceptive devices and drugs, which have greatly improved the ability of people to control their family size and avoid unwanted pregnancies. There is, of course, still a long way to go, for, as the WHO points out: 'every minute of every day and night, a woman dies because she has become pregnant', and essentially all of these deaths are in developing countries. The supply of contraceptive materials, advice, and medical assistance are thus now clearly of ongoing and critical importance. As to abortion, current responsible thinking supports the use of this only as the lesser of two evils, the greater being the birth of seriously defective children (and the majority of parents would certainly agree with this policy), and there are active endeavours to shift detection of anomalies to increasingly earlier stages—first to the preimplantation period, and so avoid establishing a defective *pregnancy*, and then into the gamete phase (until syngamy occurs), with the object of avoiding even the production of abnormal *embryos*. Constant vigilance is no doubt mandatory, but the present trend in scientific medicine is distinctly *up* the famous slope, not down.

The problems of 'competing rights'

Rights are often claimed but cannot often be granted the expected recognition. The United Nations takes note of many claims and has solemnly issued many 'Declarations', but there, for the most part, the matter rests. In the present context, we have the rights of embryos, fetuses, people, and animals—all morally persuasive but generally in competition, so that full recognition of any is impossible. Compromise is needed, and this is where contention arises.

A point often made is that human embryo experimentation would not be necessary if adequate trials were carried out with the embryos of non-human primates, and indeed that full testing with these primates should be mandatory before agents and procedures were used on human embryos. This policy is proposed as a recognition of the rights of the human embryo. On the other hand, most people would agree that such a practice is not justified unless monkeys are indeed the best available models for human beings, and often in the past they have not proven to be so. Tests employing these animals (commonly the rhesus monkey) have been standard procedure for a number of years now in the development of contraceptive agents and other drugs, and the laws of many countries require this before a new product or procedure can be licenced for human use. But the wisdom of such a stand has been seriously questioned;[183] for one drug under test, the mini-pig (a small variety well suited for laboratory work) turned out to be at least as good a model as the rhesus monkey, and the difference between the rhesus and capuchin monkeys was as great as between any other two species in the study, which included also the rat, guinea-pig, and dog. In addition, many primate species are becoming scarce in the wild, and so must be bred in captivity, which greatly increases the cost. On top of that, non-human primates turned out to be more difficult subjects for IVF+ET than human beings, and to show many differences in detail; at least until 1986, very few young monkeys, and of very few species, have been born following IVF—the baboon, the rhesus monkey, and the cynomolgous *Macaca fascicularis*;[23] there does not appear to have been any attempts with the apes.

The great bulk of prehuman testing is with laboratory animals, and these too have their rights, as sundry animal rights groups have long insisted, and there is a growing acceptance of the need for higher standards in the maintenance and use of these species, as well as the need to do without them wherever possible. While informed opinions agree that there is no prospect of our being able to dispense altogether with experimental animals for basic research, for the development of clinical applications, for drug testing, and for teaching,[184,185] proper justification is necessary for the use of animals, and firm restraint needs to be shown with the numbers used. Under these circumstances, and with the knowledge of the kind of information being sought, a proper stage at which investigations should move on from animal to human embryo has to be recognized.

As things are at present, with no fully appropriate animal model (and really no likelihood of there actually being one), some experimentation on human embryos is unavoidable if progress is to be made—we do need to know much more about the physiology of the human embryo in particular. *General* benefit could follow from this progress. Even modest improvements in the efficiency of IVF programmes could maternally reduce the current rate of embryo loss. Calculated on the basis that there are at present in the region of 1000 IVF births a year, world-wide, raising the success rate from say 10 per cent to 20 per cent per treatment cycle would 'save' at least 5000 embryos a year, in the sense that they could survive to birth. The actual number saved would be much higher, because the calculation was made on the assumption that only one embryo is transferred on each occasion, whereas in fact as many as four are commonly involved. In addition, correspondingly more infertile women would be enabled to have children. As better methods of early diagnosis are developed, there would be fewer abnormal pregnancies (natural as well as IVF) and therefore fewer spontaneous or induced abortions, and fewer defective children born. Standing in the way of these possible gains is the right to life of a relatively small number of embryos likely to be used for experimental purposes. If the decision depended upon numerical considerations and the prevailing right of the majority, the outcome would be automatic, but attribution of the right to 'utmost respect from the time of conception' virtually precludes anything in the way of experiment. The situation is highly anomalous, for embryos of the same age (i.e. preimplantation), pursuing their destinies in the oviduct or uterus, enjoy essentially no protection at all. The actual existence of an embryo in a woman's body, following a normal intercourse, is generally quite unknown to anyone, and its natural loss, signalled by a belated menstruation if implantation had begun, passes without mourning or obsequies, as also does its deliberate destruction by means of a 'morning-after' pill, IUD, dilatation and curettage, or vacuum aspiration. So the natural death of an embryo or its willful killing, when these things happen in a woman's body, fail to evoke strong reactions from Church or State, but the *use* of an embryo in ways that could bring benefits to many is condemned as morally indefensible.

As we have seen (Chapter 1, pp. 22–31), the biological facts do not accord at all with the notion that fertilization in any sense confers 'personhood', nor do they support the assignment to the preimplantation embryo of the kind of rights just considered. It was for this reason that some biologists in the UK introduced the term 'pre-embryo' or 'proembryo', pointing out that clear evidence of the future individual appeared only with the formation of the embryonic disc and primitive streak, about 14 days after fertilization.[10] These are indeed the first positive signs of the forthcoming fetus; and, importantly, such an outcome is by no means inevitable, for the embryo may proceed instead to become a 'hydatidiform mole', 'blighted ovum', or 'dropsical ovum', wherein no fetus (no 'future person') exists—instead (commonly) a cancer could threaten the life of the pregnant woman. For anyone familiar with the biological details, the argument could be convincing, but of course cannot be expected to convince everyone. There are good reasons for this. For one thing, in the minds of many non-biologists the concept of a 'beginning person' unavoidably includes the mental image of a tiny baby, complete with minute hands and feet, and it is unthinkable that such an entity should not have 'full protection'. Even if the actual nature of the embryo as an invisibly small group of a dozen or more similar cells could be envisaged, the question of its 'rights' would still be well outside the every-day sphere of thinking, and the problem of the attribution of rights at a particular stage of development an even more bewildering challenge. Under these circumstances, there is bound to be a strong inclination to follow the lead of 'appropriate' authorities on moral issues, and for many people these are under the aegis of the Church. Even biologists (and others familiar with this system of thought) may also prefer to follow such a lead, if they considered the Church to have a special mandate on questions of this kind. Yet, historically, ecclesiastical ideas about prenatal life have varied a great deal—as noted in Chapter 1, (pp. 30, 31), the start of life as marked by entry of the soul was thought, by no less a notable than St Thomas Aquinas, to occur as late as the fourth or fifth month of pregnancy. And, of course, modern Church ideas are based on biological information gained during the past century and a half, including von Baer's identification of the mammalian egg in 1827 and the elucidation of the major events of fertilization by van Beneden (rabbit), Hertwig (sea urchin), Sobotta (mouse), and others towards the end of the nineteenth century. Then, the undeniably impressive fact that fertilization initiates the cleavage sequence, provided all that was needed to establish it in ecclesiastic and popular minds as the logical point for the start of a human life. That the World Medical Association in 1949 should lend its weight to such a pronouncement was unfortunate from the biologists' point of view, but almost certainly no serious thought was given on that occasion to the possible significance of their 'declaration' for questions relating to the time of origin of the individual. Fertilization of mammalian eggs *in vitro* had yet to be attained, the prospects of human IVF+ET must have seemed very remote, the possible need for human embryo experimentation was virtually undreamed of, and genetic engineering on human embryos would have been strictly in the realm of fantasy. And so, the human embryo has come to enjoy rather special privileges.

Quite a different situation exists for the established fetus—admittedly in large part because of its nuisance value. Under English law, a pregnancy may be terminated if 'continuation of the pregnancy would involve risk to the life of the pregnant woman ... greater than if the pregnancy were terminated'. It is well recognized that continuation of any pregnancy involves greater risk than termination; that would seem to leave the fetus with no protection at all, but most doctors were prepared to interpret the law as it was presumably intended to be, and offer termination only on sound medical grounds. However, in the course of time, interpretation has become more liberal. At a recent international medical conference, the situation was summed up by an obstetrician quite simply: 'The Act provides for two doctors to allow abortion when they and the woman feel it is the best solution to her problems'. In the United States, the Supreme Court has ruled that, during the first trimester of pregnancy, a woman has a constitutional right not to have a child if she does not want it.[186]† In these countries and elsewhere, reasons for requesting an abortion have increased to include the trivial (see section on Elective Abortion on pp. 129, 130). The philosophy is reinforced by court cases in which parents claim damages from doctors for not informing them adequately about the possible birth of a defective child, thus allowing them an opportunity for abortion, and handicapped children sue doctors and even parents for 'wrongful birth'.

There are, however, indications of growing opposition to abortion, and not only that but even to antenatal diagnosis, which of course often provides the reason for abortion. The mounting feeling—which could be termed 'humane thinking'—is that even a genetically defective fetus has a right to be born and experience life outside, though it may be short and nasty, and publicity has been given to accounts by people who have wittingly become the parents of handicapped children, claiming that the experience has enriched their lives. This, of course, must depend very much on the people involved, for the necessary tolerance and dedication are not granted to everyone; so the decision not to abort a genetically defective fetus must remain one essentially for the parents to make. The change in popular outlook is already

---

†In Canada, the Supreme Court ruled on 28 January 1988 that Criminal Code prohibitions of abortion were unconstitutional.

being reflected in an increase in the frequency with which defective births are being reported.

In recent years, the rights of the fetus have become subjects of debate in rather a different connection, namely the use of fetal brain and adrenal gland tissue for the treatment of degenerative brain conditions in adults (see Chapter 2, pp. 80, 81). If the fetus is obtained following an abortion quite unconnected with its subsequent use, there can be no serious ethical objections to the procedure (though some do demur), but there is a clear possibility that the provision of material for the treatment of a relative or friend, or in frankly commercial circumstances, could prove to be an adequate motive for an induced abortion. There could, of course, also be cases of women becoming pregnant with the purpose of supplying fetal material, especially if such transplants prove to be the only effective means of treatment, and from some points of view the procedure is morally defensible if the rights of an adult person are held to prevail over those of the fetus.

Ectogenesis—possible *and* permissible?

It has long been a popular fantasy that the means might be developed for 'growing' a human being in the laboratory, turning out a fully specified product. Though generally ridiculed in the scientific community and firmly rejected by others on ethical grounds, it is yet warmly approved by some feminists as a way of freeing women from biological bondage, so the idea does merit closer inspection. This may ease some anxieties about the imminent likelihood of the procedure being employed, but it is also worth doing because some aspects are of practical medical importance, such as the extra-corporeal support of very immature infants. What then are the prospects in the foreseeable future of our being able to culture a human embryo to the stage where the fetus emerges, and then on to the point at which birth would normally take place?—some of the problems are dealt with in ref.[187] And could the product possibly prove to be a 'normal' human being in the fullest sense?

Culture of the human embryo through the earlier stages up to blastocyst expansion presents no serious difficulty and has already been done, but devising conditions that would permit the embryo to *implant* in culture and establish its important 'germ layers' under those conditions poses considerable problems, as is also the case with the embryos of rats and mice (see Chapter 2, pp. 36–41). The expansion and 'blossoming' of the embryo after it has installed itself in the uterine endometrum (Fig. 1.6) would seem to require a substrate with properties well beyond our present technical skills and knowledge to manufacture. Essentially, the reason is that the endometrium is living tissue and not a passive structure—it *responds* in an active and complex way to the burrowing embryo. How to duplicate these properties artifically is a daunting challenge.

Initially, the endometrium gets an improved blood supply and the smaller vessels, the capilliaries, become more permeable, so that oxygen, nutrients, hormones, etc., pass more readily into the tissues and so reach the embryo in increasing amounts to meet its growing needs. The numerous glands that exist in the endometrium enlarge and their secretion rate rises, providing essential materials. All these changes take place as a true *interaction* between embryo and endometrium, and do not occur, or not nearly to the same extent, if items like fragments of muscle or bone, or glass beads, are experimentally inserted (this being, of course, in the uteri of laboratory animals). In addition, as implantation proceeds, the hormonal status of the body as a whole gradually changes, the variations being necessary for successive stages of development of the embryo, which is busy elaborating the beginnings of placenta, amnion, and yolk sac.

As the embryo grows, the fetus emerges and in turn grows, and on top of that the placenta and other essential structures mature, the total mass of new tissue increases prodigiously. The uterus achieves impressive growth, too, which is evident from the fact that before implantation it is only 4×8 cm in size and weighs about 60 g, while at term it accommodates 2.5 kg or more of child plus placenta, and weighs nearly a kilogramme itself. To match these changes, the vascular supply to the uterus—arteries, veins, and lymphatics—undergoes great enlargement, and the placenta generates its own vascular system, supplying the fetus via the umbilical cord.

The anatomy and physiology of a normal pregnancy represents so vast a creation that one despairs of ever duplicating it artificially. But hope should not be lost altogether, for there is the phenomenon of 'ectopic pregnancy' (discussed in Chapter 4, p. 96), in which the embryo implants on the abdominal surface of the ovary, oviduct, uterus, or other organ. Such embryos often develop a placenta and other structures, and proceed to advanced stages of pregnancy. This is really quite astonishing, for the abdominal (peritoneal) surface of an organ is quite unlike the uterine endometrium in structure and function, and even more surprising is the research finding, made in the mouse, that an embryo transferred to the testis of a male animal was able to achieve about half of the normal extent of development, despite the 'wrong' hormonal balance, among other things. (If we may digress for a moment, it has been proposed by some male 'gay' couples that one of them might experience a pregnancy through the abdominal injection of an embryo, in the hope that the condition would continue long enough for the fetus to reach the stage of viability, when it would be removed by 'caesarian' delivery. The idea could be feasible, though approaching suicidal, owing to the high risk of haemorrhage and other problems associated with ectopic pregnancies.)

The fact that ectopic pregnancies are able to advance so far certainly indicates that *biological* makeshift arrangements can suffice to meet the needs of developing embryos and fetuses, and this does foster the belief that fabricating an artificial womb, though currently quite out of the question, could be within our technical grasp in the not-too-distant future. Attention would seem to be needed most for duplicating the tissues capable of accepting the implanting blastocyst and responding to its needs; the occurrence of ectopic pregnancy suggests that this interaction is not as specialized a function as one might have thought, though so far no-one appears to have come anywhere near constructing a functional substitute for the endometrium, despite many attempts. Once the embryo's primary implantation objectives have been achieved, simpler culture conditions could perhaps suffice—this is certainly the message to be read from Dennis New's experiments with rat embryos (see Chapter 2, pp. 38, 39)—until the sheer size of the conceptus required some sort of 'perfusion system'. Then there could be increasingly onerous adjustments to be made in meeting nutritional, respiratory, and excretory needs, and supply of hormones and other factors. Good indications of what would be required are provided by observations that have been made in attempts to sustain late human fetuses and premature infants.

The nominal duration of human pregnancy is 38—38.5 weeks, at which time the newborn should weigh at least 2.5 kg; births with less than these figures are classed as premature, and around 7–12 per cent of births are premature in a wide range of social groups. Prematurity accounts for nearly half of all deaths at about the time of birth, the mortality reaching almost 100 per cent with birth weights of 800 g or less. For any infant, however, birth is a great challenge—suddenly, it has to carry its own weight (quite an effort even when horizontal), maintain its own body temperature, breathe air (instead of amniotic fluid), consume and digest food and absorb the products, and excrete wastes. The main problem, especially with premature babies, is the breathing of air, for this requires that the surfaces of the air-sacs in the lungs do not stick together at expiration, and this in turn depends on the presence of the substance 'surfactant' (a phospholipid) on the air-sac surfaces, which normally appears shortly before birth. So, in premature babies, lack of surfactant leads to abnormal lung function, deterioration of lung tissues and the development of 'hyaline membrane disease'—a great killer. Treatment involving spraying surfactant mist into the infant's respiratory tract and injecting hormones into the mother to promote surfactant production is moderately effective. There are several other weighty problems too, including the tendency for jaundice in the newborn, but encouraging progress is being made to deal with these.[188,189]

Special apparatus was developed some years ago to help meet the needs of the premature, particularly for the purpose of short-term relief, as when a newborn fails to start breathing—often, just an hour or two's support at such a time can save the day. These procedures cannot yet be continued for much longer than an hour or two, but with further technical improvement, really long-term support could become feasible in the future. One form of this apparatus is known as the 'Klung system', the name coming from a component whose function combines those of both kidney and lung;[190] a simplified diagram shows the layout of the system (Fig. 5.1). The infant is held in an incubator, to keep its temperature at the right level, and suspended in a sort of weighing machine capable of detecting quite small changes in weight; this is done to check the rate at which blood is being transfused into and out of the infant through its umbilical vessels, the rate being adjusted to keep the weight constant. Blood leaving the infant passes through the Klung unit in which it traverses spaces between layers of special plastic sheeting, which has the property of allowing oxygen and carbon dioxide to pass back and forth, as an approximation to lung function; other sheets allow the transfer of substances like electrolytes (essential salts) and amino acids from an outside supply, in such a way as to keep a steady blood concentration, representing the kidney function. The Klung unit is a highly complex affair and its operation requires the constant attention of an experienced team, a major commitment for just one fetus or premature baby.

Would there be adequate justification for all the effort and expense involved in a large-scale operation? The baby factories ('hatcheries') in Aldous Huxley's *Brave New World* relieved

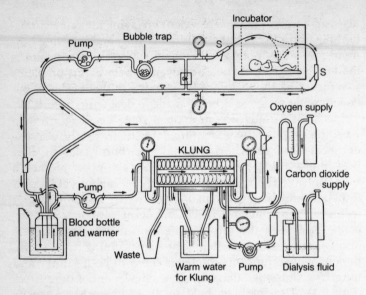

Fig. 5.1 The 'Klung' system. Blood from a premature infant is warmed, 'cleaned' (waste products removed) and has its oxygen replenished, before being returned (with careful attention to pressures). At points marked 'S', blood samples can be removed for testing. (From ref. 190.)

women of the burdens of pregnancy and nursing, and there presumably were, or could be, important advantages flowing from this. The commitment to child-bearing and rearing has effectively barred many women (in the past, at least) from realization of their personal potential, from the rewarding experience of a further education, of achieving success in business or industry, of winning acclaim in medicine or science, of reaching high political status, and so on. To this day, there are continuing inequities stemming from this source. So, for women, there could still be significant gains from ectogenesis; in addition, the method could be welcomed as an alternative preferable to the use of a brain-dead woman as a surrogate (discussed in Chapter 4, pp. 100–1). But the 'hatchery' system also enabled citizens to be produced in a controllable number and equipped in a general way for their function in life—those destined for work in the tropics were immunized during development to protect them against diseases likely to be encountered there. Later, during child-hood, they were subjected to intense training and behaviour conditioning to shape them for specific roles in the social hierarchy, and ensure that they would never wish to change. There was much more in the 'hatchery' system than ectoge-nesis, and a great deal that would not seriously appeal to many today.

The inclusion of the genetic engineering of the future in the concept of ectogenesis could offer many advantages. Already, viruses have been reconstructed to enable them to introduce a chosen gene into genetically defective animals, thus effectively 'curing' the condition, and there is every reason to anticipate that this technique will be applicable to human subjects eventually. In the fullness of time it should be possible to deal in this way with all human genetic defects, and if and when this ambitious goal is achieved, and since most nutritional and infectious diseases have been elimin-ated, or are on their way out, we could be lucky enough one day to be able to claim that *all* our children are born healthy and, barring accidents and misadventure, should remain that way for a generous life-span. This seems a wholly worthy and indeed *ethically imperative* aim, so it is strange to hear of proposals to bring in legislation to stop the development of these genetic techniques. The reason appears to be a deep-rooted concern that getting rid of all *genetic* defects smacks of 'eliteism'—the fear that a myopic programme of eugenics would take control, arousing the sort of anxieties that were discussed in relation to 'dehumanization'—a eugenic drive, not just for healthy people, but for 'superior' people and eventually for a 'master race'. It is not at all clear, however, how this could possibly be done. We know about nearly all genes only from what happens when they are missing or defective, so all we can reasonably hope to do at present is to restore the *normal*. Certainly, it should be possible also to produce a larger than normal human being, to judge from the reports on the much larger than normal mouse (see Chapter 2, pp. 54, 55), but mere size is by no means everything. Robert Wadlow reached a height of 272 cm (8 ft 11.1 in), but that feature really only secured him a mention in the *Guinness Book of Records*. To be a 'superman' would require many other attributes, and most of these, such as intelligence, would depend on a complex interaction of genes, together with various environmental effects (see Table 5.1—even identical twins can show big differences if reared apart). The fear that ectogenesis coupled with genetic engineering would result in the production of a 'master race' does not appear, at present, to be well founded.

Problems of legal control

The areas of concern here are: artificial insemination—donor (no longer abbreviated to AID because of possible confusion

Table 5.1. Degrees of association (correlation coefficients) between the IQ ratings of people related in different ways and living in similar or different environments[191]

		0.00	0.10	0.20	0.30	0.40	0.50	0.60	0.70	0.80	0.90
Unrelated persons	Reared apart	▬▬▬▬▬									
	Reared together		▬▬▬								
Foster-parent–child				▬▬▬							
Parent–child				▬▬▬▬▬▬▬							
Siblings	Reared apart				▬						
	Reared together				▬▬▬▬▬						
Two-egg twins	Opposite sex						▬▬				
	Like sex						▬▬▬▬				
One-egg twins	Reared apart								▬		
	Reared together								▬▬▬		

The horizontal bars represent the ranges of observed values

with AIDS); the test-tube baby procedure or IVF+ET (including sperm, egg, and embryo donation); surrogacy; genetic engineering (or recombinant DNA technology); and elective abortion. Only points that appeal as salient are discussed here, for numerous detailed treatments have appeared in recent years. [21,174,176,192–7]

Artificial insemination—donor [198]

Major responsibilities of the doctor are to take care that no infection is passed on to the patient from the donor, and also that the risk of inbreeding is avoided by making sure that donor and recipient are not close relatives. Both these requirements mean that the doctor needs to keep a detailed register of his donors, noting both their medical history and family relationships. Mishaps in either of these areas could become grounds for litigation.

It is important that the woman who is inseminated gives her written consent, for obvious reasons, and it is advisable, though not so critically important, that the husband should do so too. In most jurisdictions, children born from donor insemination were inevitably labelled illegitimate (unless the husband was prepared to commit perjury), and commonly this problem was overcome by the couple formally adopting the child. To do that, required the consent of the semen donor, who would then have to become known, thus destroying the incognito generally thought to be a necessary part of the arrangement. This difficulty was overcome by some doctors by mixing the semen from two or more donors, and also adding what semen the husband could produce, so that paternity could not be established unequivocally. Nowadays, in some legislations, the question of paternity is settled by the law declaring the husband to be the father 'by presumption', this statement being non-rebuttable. This has become necessary, as well as convenient, because biological paternity can be established with a high degree of confidence by the technique of 'DNA fingerprinting'—individual identities can be recognized from the pattern of distinctive DNA repetitive sequences, which can be ascertained from a drop of blood or semen, or a single hair-root.[199] Lacking these legal and scientific devices, a donor's identity could be revealed often by exercise of a child's right to know his biological father, and the donor might then be held responsible for maintenance of the child—or, if these manoeuvres failed, the doctor himself might be legally bound to provide maintenance.

In an active insemination programme, it is natural that sooner or later a child is born with a congenital defect—even with well-selected donors and no history of hereditary problems in the inseminated woman's family. Under these circumstances, a charge of professional negligence might be based on the allegation that enquiry into the donor's family history was inadequate or that mishandling of the semen was responsible. Expert witness by a professional geneticist might then be called for.

Sometimes ill-effect is associated with the treatment with gonadotrophic hormones, administration of which may be considered necessary to ensure that ovulation takes place at about the same time as the insemination, so that prospects of fertilization are good. To avoid this risk, several inseminations may be made around the time of ovulation (estimated by blood hormone assay), and recognition of a preovulatory follicle may be possible with the aid of ultrasound scanning or NMR imaging.

IVF+ET

There are still major differences of opinion on just what means should be used to control the medical and biological procedures constituting or potentially supplementary to IVF+ET. In some jurisdictions, there are stringent legislative measures, backed by criminal sanctions, while in others regulation of all activities depends upon a voluntary code of conduct. There are reasons to prefer the latter system.[195,197]

These include the fact that the methods used are continually being changed and often improved (see Chapter 4, pp. 94–9), while legislation tends to be relatively inflexible and thus likely to become outdated. The main features thought to require statutory control are:

1. The prohibition against fertilization between animal and human gametes. There is, however, the highly valued 'hamster egg penetration test' for helping in the diagnosis of infertility in men (Chapter 3, p. 91); the prospects of extensive development ensuing are virtually nil, but some people may detect here the 'thin end of a wedge', and so object on principle.

2. The adequate trial or consideration of other possible remedies before IVF+ET is embarked upon. This would appear to be common sense, and several more conservative measures can certainly be considered, such as those identified as DIPI and GIFT (Chapter 4, pp. 94–9).

3. The provision by the couple of evidence that they are formally married, and consent to the projected treatment. The need for consent is hardly likely to cause dissension, but opinions are certainly divided on the subject of marital status, where perhaps regulations concerning adoption can provide suitable guidance. Whether lesbian couples should be assisted into parenthood, with the aid of donor semen, probably has few protagonists, though much of the opposition may be attributable to prejudice; from the resulting child's point of view, the arrangement could be entirely satisfactory. For a 'gay' couple, on the other hand, the proposition, involving donated embryos and a theoretically possible ectopic pregnancy, could be firmly excluded, if only because of the risk to life of the recipient (see Chapter 4, p. 96).

4. The performance of the IVF+ET procedure in approved clinical premises and by approved medical staff. These conditions seem wholly acceptable, an important point being that 'clinical' and not 'hospital' facilities are specified, the latter involving unjustifiable expense, unless medical complications were anticipated.

5. The establishment of an independent ethical committee whose approval is required for any variations in technical procedures, especially if calculated to impair the embryo's capacity for full normal development. Difficulties here are twofold: the ethical committee may feel bound to permit no risks at all, and so forbid any deviation from established procedures, a policy that could preclude the adoption of important improvements, or it may feel partisan to the clinical team, and so approve proposed moves incurring major risks to embryos or patient, if a successful outcome could win wide acclaim. Indeed, it is scarcely possible to steer a middle course consistently.

6. The keeping of detailed and proper records. There should be no argument here.

Opinions differ widely on the subject of experimentation on human embryos. In Victoria, Australia, the relevant sections of the Infertility (Medical Procedures) Act 1984 became law in August 1986, and these allow experimentation on embryos in the first 14 days of pregnancy, subject to the approval of an ethical committee. Because of consistent failure to obtain such approval, the medical community concerned arranged for the Infertility (Medical Procedures) (Amendment) Bill to be brought forward in 1987; this was designed to permit experimentation on the human *egg*, after sperm penetration but before completion of the fertilization process at 'syngamy', union of chromosome groups. Such a preparation is, by definition, not a *fertilized* egg and certainly not an embryo, and yet could yield useful information on both the maternal and paternal chromosomal status, as well as on the capacity for fertilization. Some objections, however, were raised even to this proposal.

A rather intractable problem is presented by embryos produced in an IVF+ET programme in excess of the number required for return to the patient. Prospects for establishing a pregnancy appear to be optimal following the insertion of three or perhaps four embryos, provided these are of good quality, i.e. cleaving regularly and of normal appearance, but to obtain this number it is necessary to begin with several more, because of the uncertainties of fertilization and early development. If more than four embryos eventuate, it becomes necessary to decide on the fate of the extra or 'spare' embryos. Generally, these are regarded as being the 'property' of the couple under treatment, and they can be donated to another couple or cryopreserved for use should the pregnancy attempt prove to be unsuccessful. If this pregnancy does prove fruitful the 'owners' may request a second pregnancy, or donate the embryos to another couple or to the clinic for use in research, if that course of action is not against regulations. Alternatively, contact with the couple may be lost for one reason or another, whereupon the clinic is faced with having to make the decision—donation, research, or destruction—and it is possible that suitable recipients may be lacking and both of the other courses of action are specifically forbidden by the law. A few clinics try to avoid this dilemma by returning all embryos that develop; occasionally, this method produces a dangerously large multiple pregnancy, whereupon fetuses above a certain number are 'terminated' by heart puncture, which many people could regard as ethically unacceptable procedure.

Fertilization of the eggs can be made with sperm from the husband, if he can provide them, or from a donor, in which case considerations are similar to those set out above in the section on *Artificial insemination—donor*. Eggs may be donated by another woman, fertilized with the husband's sperm and then transferred, or embryos can be donated and transferred; in neither case is there any likely legal difficulty over parenthood (generally speaking, the law considers the woman giving birth to be the mother), though the child may later claim the right to know its genetic mother.

Surrogacy

The idea of surrogacy is 'as old as the hills': in *Genesis* xvi, 1–4, we are told how Abram's wife, being infertile, asked

Abram to go to her maid, for 'it may be that I obtain children by her'; then in xxx, 1–5, Jacob's wife, also being infertile, asked Jacob to cohabit with her maid—both maids duly bore children on behalf of their mistresses.

In the modern context, there are several variations on the theme (but without the extra-marital intercourse) depending on whether a couple provides both sperm and eggs (or sperm or eggs, with the help of a fourth party), or only embryos, for the establishment of pregnancy in a surrogate. Legal problems arise when the surrogate refuses to part with the child after birth, and courts are often reluctant to force her to do this, even though she may have been under formal contract. Many jurisdictions regard the woman giving birth as the mother, *ipso facto*, even if it did all start with someone else's egg or embryo. Or she may demand additional payment at this stage. Alternatively, the couple may refuse to accept the child, or to make any outstanding payment, if the child is genetically handicapped, is of the 'wrong' sex, or has an odd appearance, or because they have separated since the pregnancy was founded. Then, again, where adoption is necessary to formalize relations between the child and the couple, it can happen that the couple are both above the legal age for foster parents. Because of difficulties like these, and also because surrogacy is regarded as highly subject to commercial exploitation, any involvement of advertising or of a 'contract', or the help of paid intermediaries, is commonly forbidden, and even the procedure itself may be declared illegal.

These measures could reasonably be regarded as needlessly draconian, for there plainly can be circumstances (as, for instance, when a woman's infertility is due to congenital lack of the uterus or to hysterectomy for cervical cancer) when a pregnancy is not possible and yet the couple hopes for a child with the normal parent–child genetic relationship, rather than adopt an unrelated infant, so that a surrogacy arrangement would be the best, indeed the only, solution.[170] There are instances in which a member of the immediate family has helped out in this way—recent cases include a sister, a mother, and even a grandmother. Here, financial reward was presumably not expected, but if the surrogate is quite unrelated, some sort of reward, in addition to insurance against risk, is surely justified. The proceedings could be under the control of something having the legal status of an adoption society, which could also serve as a kind of clearing house, with a dossier of women prepared to function as surrogates and found to be suitable for the task, and such a service would need some measure of publicity. Alternatives to total prohibition do merit careful consideration.

Genetic engineering

Legislation, enacted or impending, appears to be wholly opposed to any attempted application of genetic engineering with human embryos, and this is indeed well justified with the technology in its present state of development (as described in Chapter 2, pp. 50–60), though the future prospects are undeniably bright. Indeed, one could reasonably claim that the use of recombinant DNA technology in the early diagnosis of sex and certain genetic defects is already playing an important role—with strong legal connections (see this chapter, pp. 113–15), but it is the possibility of treatment and cure that is most alluring, though as yet unattainable.

Elective abortion

There seems to be general agreement in legal circles that prevention of implantation of the embryo is not to be treated as equivalent to abortion, and so the use of IUDs, 'morning-after' pills, menstrual regulation, and 'D & C' treatment are all in the clear. However, the Law is strongly invoked in the control of later terminations (see this chapter, pp. 113–15), where public concern initially had to do with *restricting* the practice of abortion, but now seems to be in the process of making a complete volte-face. This chiefly concerns moves to uphold the rights and wishes of parents and the rights of (even unborn) children, in circumstances where medical advisers and their associates can be said to have renegued on their duties, either by failing to advise properly or by failing to terminate an abnormal pregnancy or *both*. In these respects, litigation has of late become highly complicated, especially in the USA (an illuminating account appears in ref. 196). Lawsuits have been filed for the following reasons (among many others):

(1) failure to offer amniocentesis (and subsequently abortion) to a pregnant woman over 35 years of age (her child turned out to be a case of Down's syndrome);

(2) failure to take appropriate action despite knowledge of possible rhesus incompatibility (the child was severely handicapped);

(3) the clinical laboratory wrongly reported that tests showed no evidence of either parent being a carrier of Tay–Sachs disease (the child exhibited the condition);

(4) all tests applied during pregnancy failed to reveal that the child was due to develop Duchenne muscular dystrophy;

(5) as the husband was known to be a carrier of a genetic disease, he was given a vasectomy, but later a child was born with the hereditary defect.

Increasingly, too, children have sued 'for pain and suffering' endured through being born with a genetic defect, as in case (3) above, or to the lack of appropriate treatment for the mother, as in case (2) above. As yet, in American courts, children are not permitted to sue their parents, but this may soon change as courts come to give more weight to the principle that parents owe a real responsibility to their unborn children.

6

Synopsis

Fertility consists in the production of eggs and sperm that can take part in fertilization. At fertilization, the egg receives a stimulus that causes it to start dividing, first into two cells, then into four, then eight, and so on, a process known as cleavage. Soon a round mass of cells is formed (the morula) and this hollows out to constitute the blastocyst, which becomes attached to the endometrium lining the inside of the uterus; the blastocyst then embeds itself completely in the endometrium in the process of implantation. Embryonic and fetal development take place in sequence, the uterus enlarging to accommodate the greatly increased size of the fetus, with birth as the culmination.

Eggs and sperm are both single cells, and in both the chromosome number has been reduced to half of the standard value (half of the 'diploid number') in the process of meiosis which occurs during their formation. At fertilization, the two chromosome complements come together and so restore the diploid number. The contribution of the sperm's chromosomes is the means whereby the paternal genes become incorporated in the embryo, and this is the basis of biparental inheritance.

In the *normal* course of events, human reproduction involves huge losses. From some 7 million or so primordial germ cells and oogonia that exist in the fetal ovary, only about 500 oocytes will eventually be ovulated, to reach the oviduct and have a chance of fertilization; many fewer will in fact be fertilized, and only an average of five infants will be born and survive; odds against, about 1 400 000:1. Spontaneous terminations in *early* pregnancy are often as high as 65 per cent, most occurring unnoticed. A large proportion of pregnancy losses is attributable to genetic defects and diseases, and only 2–3 per cent of newborn infants exhibit such anomalies (which yet means that, in the world as a whole, about 130 000 000 defective children are born each year).

Fertilization does not confer genetic uniqueness—this is achieved as a consequence of the first meiotic division, which takes place just before ovulation. Nor does fertilization mark the start of individuality—this begins much earlier, when the primordial germ cells and oogonia cease division, the nuclei pass into a resting state, and the cells thus become the oocytes. Each oocyte represents the start of an entity that persists (without cell division, except for polar body formation) to the point of formation of the fetal primordium (the embryonic disc), and continues as a unit to the birth of the infant, unless the embryonic disc splits up to form twins, triplets, etc. The acquisition of 'humanness' during development is a gradual process—nothing distinctive appears before implantation of the embryo at 7 or 8 days, and then the cells that will form a future *person*, as distinct from placenta, fetal membranes, etc., differentiate and become identifiable by 14 days. A pulsating vesicle, the forerunner of the heart, appears by 21 days, the earliest nerve-muscle reflex response can probably be evoked at 30–40 days, electrical activity in the brain can be detected first at about 12 weeks, and 'quickening' is commonly experienced by the mother at 4–5 months. Which particular stage should be regarded as the beginning of 'a person's' life is a matter of opinion. There are also differences of opinion in the Church as to when 'ensoulment' occurs. Historically, too, there were similar differences, St Augustine holding that the soul entered the body (the egg) together with the sperm, whereas for St Thomas Aquinas the likely time was at 'quickening' (at 4–5 months of pregnancy), and according to a possible interpretation of *Exodus* xxi, 22–23, it had to be some time during the recognizable period of pregnancy. A modern view is that entry of the soul, which being unique is indivisible, must be after the possibility of twinning has past—possibly at about 20 days of pregnancy.

Of more pragmatic significance are the *relative rights* of embryos, fetuses, people, and animals, which are discussed later.

Human embryos, like those of mice and rats, can readily be grown in culture in the laboratory, at least up to the blastocyst stage, but become progressively disorganized after that. Rat embryos and fetuses have been dissected out of the uterine tissue at various times after implantation and grown in culture for 1–4 days. Development appeared to be normal but was strictly limited in duration, especially in the later stages, owing to the technical difficulty of supplying the fetus with sufficient oxygen and removing the wastes, let alone providing sufficient nutrients and other factors. At the other end of pregnancy, premature human infants are being 'rescued' at increasingly earlier stages by improvements in medication and care, but to be able to support human embryos and fetuses right through pregnancy to 'birth' in culture many very difficult problems will need to be overcome.

Of more immediate interest is the fact that certain cell lines can be grown from mouse blastocysts and maintained in culture more or less indefinitely, without losing their normal character, and when introduced into another blastocyst they can take part in a normal way in the development of the recipient, participating in the production of apparently any tissue. Identified as ES or 'embryonic stem' cell lines, corresponding products could conceivably prove to be of value in the treatment of human genetic diseases.

Chimeras can be produced by putting together in culture two or more embryos, which promptly fuse and, after insertion into a foster mother, give rise eventually to a single viable young animal. The different cell populations remain distinct, so that the animal or person concerned is a mosaic of features, but any diffusible products, such as hormones, deriving from one cell population may affect the whole animal. Thus, making a chimera can be effective in correcting for the deficiencies of some embryos—by this means, cells of a parthenogenetic embryo can come to contribute to the tissues of an adult animal (including the germ line), whereas the parthenogenetic embryo on its own would not be likely to develop much beyond the stage of implantation.

Hybrids occur abundantly in nature, and can be produced artificially by encouraging animals of different species to mate, or by means of cross-insemination, probably the most famous example being the mule. Some attempts at hybridization, however, have consistently failed, such as between rabbit and hare, ferret and mink, and sheep and goat—fertilization often occurred, but embryonic development did not go far. Among the primates, hybrids are known between different species of gibbon, but there do not appear to be any records of hybrids between the higher apes or between apes and human beings.

Frogs can be 'cloned' by introducing nuclei from tadpoles into eggs whose nuclei have been destroyed by irradiation, or removed. The huge number of adults that could potentially develop would be genetically identical to the tadpole donor. Despite many attempts, no-one was able to do anything like this in mammals, but recently some success has been signalled following nuclear transfer between sheep embryos and enucleated eggs, so that there could be a prospect of being able to produce large numbers of sheep of identical genotype. Earlier work has shown that it was possible to get several 'identical twin' rabbits by separating the cells of early cleavage embryos and placing these in separate zonas, as many as eight young rabbits being produced in this way.

Parthenogenetic development (in which fertilization is lacking) is known in lizards as a normal reproductive process, and in turkeys and other birds as an occasional feature. All attempts to produce parthenogenesis in mammals have failed so far.

Low-temperature storage (cryopreservation) at $-196\,^{\circ}\text{C}$ of sperm, eggs, and embryos of some animals and human beings is now routine, and the period of possible storage appears to be virtually indefinite for at least a major proportion of the treated items. Births of human infants deriving from frozen eggs or embryos appear to be quite normal. There is no evidence of developmental defect arising from cryopreservation, and indeed during the frozen period the tissues are partially protected from the effects of ionizing radiations. The cryopreservation of both human eggs and embryos gives rise to some ethical problems.

There are rather a large number of congenital and inherited defects to which human beings are subject, many of which cause death during embryonic and fetal development, others being responsible for disability and premature death in children and adults. Chromosomal disorders can take several different forms, the one most commonly known being 'trisomy-21', which is responsible for the condition known as Down's syndrome. Women who become pregnant at the age of 30 or more are increasingly liable to give birth to an afflicted child. Inherited traits and diseases are commonly grouped according to whether the defective gene is on the X- or Y-chromosome (very nearly all of these are on the X) and according to whether the gene is dominant or recessive—well over 200 examples of X-linked recessive disorders are known, and these are expressed only in males. Most likely to be amenable to genetic engineering are the single-gene disorders, of which more than 3000 are known. In other diseases and defects, not only several genes but also environmental factors are jointly responsible. Much can be done to prevent the birth of children suffering from congenital or inherited defects by means of interviews with prospective parents and advice as to the choice of elective abortion or the use of donor semen (or, in the case of X-linked recessive traits, the removal of Y-bearing sperm from the husband's semen, which will avoid the birth of males, though this is not yet a reliable procedure). In addition, the sperm in the husband's semen can be examined for the presence of chromosomal translocations and inversions by means of the 'hamster egg penetration test', and tests can also be made on the wife's oocytes by the use of DNA probes on the chromosomes of the second polar body, which could pick up such things as trisomy-21.

From early-cleavage-stage embryos and blastocysts, 'biopsy' samples could be taken for analysis without seriously prejudicing the developmental prospects of the embryo (as judged from work on laboratory and agricultural animals), and such tests could reveal incipient developmental errors, but this procedure is not at present regarded as ethically acceptable with human embryos. After implantation, a great deal of information can be gained through the use of 'chorion villus biopsy' at 8–12 weeks of pregnancy or 'amniocentesis' at 16–18 weks of pregnancy, and later on much useful data can be obtained by means of ultrasonography, radiography, NMR imaging, and fetoscopy.

The burgeoning branch of biology known as 'genetic engineering' or recombinant DNA technology offers tremendous possibilities in the diagnosis, amelioration, and cure of human genetic diseases. By this means, diagnosis of genetic disorders can be made on human sperm, eggs, and embryos before implantation, as well as on fetal tissues in the first or second trimester of pregnancy. Symptoms shown by defective infants at birth can often be relieved by administration of hormones or other agents produced by recombinant DNA technology, and there are prospects of treating blood disorders by introducing genes into bone marrow. The possibilities of curing genetic disorders by inserting normal versions of defective genes into embryos are being actively investigated in animals, and some success has been achieved, but this procedure is not suitable for human use because of the considerable risks involved.

Experimentation on human embryos has been met with such strong opposition in some quarters that thought should be given to what advantages, if any, might be obtained by continuing with this practice. To begin with, of course, there is the prospect of improving techniques of all the manoeuvres that are involved in IVF+ET—recovery of eggs, fertilization, culture of embryos (if that is included), replacement in the oviduct, etc. With something like 1000 IVF births a year occurring now, and only between 10 and 20 per cent as the average success rate, improvements in methodology could mean avoiding the loss of two or three thousand embryos a year. Then, if advantage is to be taken of the rapidly growing field of recombinant DNA technology, many more tests will need to be made, but of course in this highly exploratory area a great deal of experimentation must be done first with laboratory animals. Early approaches in human subjects are most likely with methods that involve tissues removed from the body and replaced after treatment and testing. Suitable tissue includes bone marrow, and the model experiment in mice has already proved successful. Methods of genetic engineering have also been used in the production of a number of hormones and other biologically active substances under laboratory conditions.

A frequent need is to ascertain the sex of a child before birth, mainly as a guide to identifying those with genetic traits and diseases; this can be done by several different methods—by chromosome analysis, detection of the H–Y antigen, detection of X-linked enzymes, recognition of the 'sex chromatin', and detection of 'Y-specific DNA sequences'.

Infertility in women is most often due to hormonal irregularities or to the damaging effects of bacterial infections of the oviduct and ovary; in men, the main problem is failure to produce sufficient numbers of normal sperm, which can be due to dietary defects, infections, or hereditary factors, but often the cause cannot be ascertained. In the woman, hormone deficiencies can usually be corrected by the appropriate administration, infections by antibiotic treatment, and actual tissue damage by surgical repair. Other remedies include the use of the test-tube baby technique, or one of the variants— GIFT (introducing both sperm and eggs into the oviduct), PROST (placing pronuclear-stage eggs in the oviduct), or modifications of these methods for both technical and ethical reasons. If the husband is producing too few sperm to achieve fertility by sexual intercourse, ejaculates can be concentrated by centrifugation and the sperm delivered by artificial insemination or by injection into the abdominal cavity (a device that can also be effective when the wife's infertility is due to 'hostile' cervical mucus), or the sperm can be used for IVF or the GIFT procedure. If these measures fail, recourse may be had to the use of donor eggs or sperm, in either the IVF or GIFT settings, or donor embryos may be sought. A further option is the surrogate arrangement, though this is often hedged about with ethical and legal problems, or alternatively adoption may be considered.

There is no doubt that doctors and scientists immersed in the technology of genetic engineering and assisted reproduction are prone to become victims of what has been called a 'therapeutic imperative', which impels them to strive for the elimination of all ills and so achieve the eugenic goal of 'faultless people', without any great concern about the cost in certain human values. One moral philosopher has presented a body of evidence to show that doctors and scientists are already evincing a kind of 'dehumanization', forgetful of the traditional Medicine with its emphasis on human compassion and care, and prepared instead to 'administer death' in the forms of embryo selection and the induction of abortion. He maintains that this policy is disturbingly reminiscent of the frame of mind that distinguished the protagonists of the Nazi regime, with their avowed aim to create the 'perfect race', and their total disregard for the rights and lives of other nationals. The argument is thought-provoking, especially in view of the data assembled, but in fact the weight of evidence clearly indicates a steady upgrading in moral and ethical standards, not deterioration.

The rights of nations seem inevitably to be in competition, and this is true too for the rights of embryos, fetuses, people, and animals. The testing of drugs and manipulative procedures on animals before their use for human subjects is in general mandatory, and indeed indispensible, but is the target of fierce opposition from animal rights groups. The practice is also open to criticism because the findings are often of dubious applicability to human beings. The rights of infertile couples, like the rights of all patients, include the right to receive effective treatment. Methods of treatment for infertility are still greatly in need of improvement, and this depends heavily on embryo experimentation, particularly when the treatment takes the form of *in vitro* fertilization and embryo storage and transfer. Better methods would additionally mean reduction in the present large wastage of embryos in IVF programmes. Restriction or prohibition of human embryo experimentation, on the grounds that the embryo merits full protection from the time of fertilization, thus virtually precludes improvement of methods. By contrast, the rights of the fetus are often disregarded, with abortion being performed for trivial reasons or simply 'on request'.

Ectogenesis, the culture of human embryos and fetuses through to the time of birth, faces many difficulties for its realization, which is not likely to be for many years yet. When feasible, the system could be warmly welcomed by many women, because it could provide an opportunity for them to enjoy as full a public or professional life as most men do, and still produce a family. Ectogenesis could also provide an alternative to surrogacy, avoiding many of the ethical and legal problems of that method. Finally, ectogenesis could make an ideal environment for the application of genetic engineering, which, contrary to fears often expressed by members of the public, would not 'open the door' to the irresponsible production of 'monsters'. We know of the existence of nearly all genes by what happens when they are lacking or defective, so that appropriate gene insertion can produce a 'normal', but not a 'new creation'. In the fullness of time, genetic engineering could enable us to eliminate most genetic defects from the human race, much as we are in the process of doing with diseases due to parasites, bacteria, and viruses.

A major improvement in some legislations relating to artificial insemination with donor's semen is the practice of 'presuming' the husband to be the father of any child born, such a presumption being non-rebuttable, though actual paternity can now be determined with a high degree of confidence by means of 'DNA fingerprinting'. With IVF+ET, the most contentious aspects of litigation relate to the nature of control over experimentation on the embryo. Problems arise also with embryo storage by means of cryopreservation, and there is much disagreement on the issues raised. The smooth working of surrogacy still depends much on the goodwill of the surrogate; in some legislations, surrogacy is forbidden altogether.

References

References marked with an asterisk (*) are intended for a non-specialist readership.

1. Johnson, M. H. and Everitt, B. J. (1980). *Essential reproduction*. Blackwell Scientific Publications, Oxford.
2. Harper, M. J. K. (1982). Sperm and egg transport. In *Reproduction in mammals*, 1. *Germ cells and fertilization*, 2nd edn (eds C. R. Austin and R. V. Short), pp. 102–27. Cambridge University Press, Cambridge.
3. Yanagimachi, R. (1981). Mechanisms of fertilization in mammals. In *Fertilization and embryonic development* in vitro (eds L. Mastroianni and J. D. Biggers), pp. 81–182. Plenum Press, New York and London.
4. Yanagimachi, R. (1988). Mammalian fertilization. In *The physiology of reproduction* (eds E. Knobil and J. Neill), pp. 135–85. Raven Press, New York.
5. Plachot, M., Junca, A.-M., Mandelbaum, J., de Grouchy, J., Salat-Baroux, J., and Cohen, J. (1986). Chromosome investigations in early life. I. Human oocytes recovered in an IVF programme. *Human Reproduction* **1**, 547–51.
6. Austin, C. R. Preimplantation development. (in press). in *Marshall's physiology of reproduction*, 4th edn, Vol. 3 (ed. G. E. Lamming). Churchill Livingston, Edinburgh.
7. Mesrogli, M., Schneider, J., and Maas, D. H. A. (1988). Early pregnancy factor as a marker for the earliest stages of pregnancy in infertile women. *Human Reproduction* **3**, 113–15.
8. McLaren, A. (1972). The embryo. In *Reproduction in mammals* 2. Embryonic and fetal development, pp. 1–42. (eds C. R. Austin and R. V. Short). Cambridge University Press, Cambridge.
9. Arey, L. B. (1965). *Developmental anatomy*. W. B. Saunders, Philadelphia and London.
*10. McLaren, A. (1986). Why study early human development? *New Scientist*, 24 April, 49–52.
*11. McLaren, A. (1987). Can we diagnose genetic disease in pre-embryos? *New Scientist*, 10 December, 42–7.

12. Rhodes, P. (1969). *Reproductive physiology for medical students*. J. & A. Churchill, London.

13. Potter, F. L. (1961). *Pathology of the fetus and the infant*, 2nd edn. Year Book Medical Publishers, Chicago.

14. Short, R. V. (1979). When a conception fails to become a pregnancy. In *Maternal recognition of pregnancy*, Ciba Foundation Symposium 64 (N.S.), pp. 377–94. Excerpta Medica, Amsterdam.

15. Edwards, R. G. (1986). Causes of early embryonic loss in human pregnancy. *Human Reproduction* **1**, 185–98.

16. Plachot, M., Junca, A.-M., Mandelbaum, J., de Grouchy, J., Salat-Baroux, J., and Cohen, J. (1987). Chromosome investigations in early life. II. Human preimplantation embryos. *Human Reproduction* **2**, 29–35.

17. Plachot, M., de Grouchy, J., M., Junca, A.-M., Mandelbaum, J., Salat-Baroux, J., and Cohen, J. (1988). Chrosome analysis of human oocytes and embryos: does delayed fertilization increase chromosome imbalance? *Human Reproduction* **3**, 125–7.

18. Baker, T. G. (1982). Oogenesis and ovulation. In *Reproduction in mammals*, 2nd edn (eds C. R. Austin and R. V. Short) 1. *Germ cells and fertilization*, pp. 17–45. Cambridge University Press, Cambridge.

*19. M. Warnock (Chairman) (1984). *Report of the Committee of Enquiry into Human Fertilization and Embryology*. H.M. Stationery Office, London.

20. Dunstan, G. R. (1983). Social and ethical aspects. In *Developments in human reproduction and their eugenic, ethical implications* (ed. C. O. Carter), pp. 213–226. Academic Press, London.

*21. Williams, G. (1958). *The sanctity of life and the criminal law*. Faber & Faber, London.

*22. Singer, P. and Wells, D. (1984). *The reproduction revolution*. Oxford University Press, Oxford.

23. Bavister, B. D. (1986). Animal *in vitro* fertilization and embryo development. In *Manipulation of mammalian development*. 4. *Developmental biology* (ed. R. B. L. Gwatkin), Vol. 4, pp. 81–148. Plenum Press, New York.

24. Beier, H. M. and Lindner, H. R. (eds) (1983). *Fertilization of the human egg* in vitro. Springer-Verlag, Berlin.

25. Wood, C. and Trounson, A. (eds) (1984). *Clinical in vitro fertilization*. Springer-Verlag, Berlin and New York.

26. Steptoe, P.C. and Edwards, R.G. (1978). Birth after the re-implantation of a human embryo. *Lancet* **ii**, 316.

27. New, D.A.T. (1983). *In vitro* culture of embryo and fetus. In *Developments in human reproduction and their eugenic, ethical implications* (ed. C.O. Carter), pp. 163–76. Academic Press, London.

28. New, D.A.T. (1978). Whole-embryo culture and the study of mammalian embryos during organogenesis. *Biological Reviews* **53**, 81–122.

29. McLaren, A. (1976). *Mammalian chimaeras*. Cambridge University Press, Cambridge.

30. McLaren, A. (1981). Mammalian chimaeras. In *Well-being of mankind and genetics* (ed. D.K. Belyaev), pp. 142–50. M.I.R. Publishers, Moscow.

31. Tarkowski, A.K. (1961). Mouse chimaeras developed from fused eggs. *Nature* **190**, 857–60.

32. Gardner, R.L. (1968). Mouse chimaeras obtained by the injection of cells into the blastocyst. *Nature* **220**, 596.

33. Mintz, B. and Illmensee, K. (1975). Normal genetically mosaic mice produced from malignant teratocarcinoma cells. *Proceedings of the National Academy of Sciences (Washington)* **72**, 3385–9.

34. Fehilly, C.B. and Willadsen, S.M. (1986). Embryo manipulation in farm animals. In *Oxford reviews of reproductive biology*, (ed. J. Clark), Vol. 8, pp. 379–413. Oxford University Press, Oxford.

35. Polzin, V.J., Anderson, D.L., Anderson, G.B., BonDurant, R.H., Butler, J.E., Pashen, R.L., Penedo, M.C.T. and Rowe, J.D. Production of sheep–goat chimeras by inner cell mass transplantation. *Journal of Animal Science* **65**, 325–30 (1987).

36. Gray, A.P. (1954). *Mammalian hybrids*. Commonwealth Agricultural Bureaux, Farnham Royal, Bucks. U.K.

37. Benirschke, K. (ed.) (1967). Sterility and fertility of interspecific mammalian hybrids. In *Comparative aspects of reproductive failure*, pp. 218–34. Springer-Verlag, New York.

38. Chang, M.C. and Hancock, J.L. (1967). Experimental hybridization. In *Comparative aspects of reproductive failure* (ed. K. Benirschke), pp. 206–17. Springer-Verlag, New York.

39. Yanagimachi, R., Yanagimachi, H., and Rogers, B.J. (1976). The use of zona-free animal ova as a test system for the assess-

ment of the fertilizing capacity of human spermatozoa. *Biology of Reproduction* **15**, 471–6.

40. Bodmer, W. F. and Cavalli-Sforza, L. L. (1976). *Genetics, evolution and man*. W. H. Freeman, San Francisco.

41. Reik, W., Collick, A., Norris, M. L., Barton, S. C., and Surani, M. A. (1987). Genetic imprinting determines methylation of parental alleles in transgenic mice. *Nature* **328**, 248–51.

42. Sapienza, C., Peterson, A. C., Rossant, J., and Balling, R. (1987). Degree of methylation of transgenes is dependent on gamete of origin. *Nature* **328**, 251–4.

43. Kaufman, M. H. (1983). *Early mammalian development: Parthenogenetic studies*. Cambridge University Press, Cambridge.

44. Briggs, R. and King, T. J. (1952). Transplantation of living nuclei from blastula cells into enucleated frogs' eggs. *Proceedings of the National Academy of Sciences (Washington)* **38**, 455–63.

45. Gurdon, J. B. (1968). Transplanted nuclei and cell differentiation. *Scientific American* **219**, 24–35.

46. Willadsen, S. M. (1986). Nuclear transplantation in sheep embryos. *Nature* **320**, 63–5.

47. Anonymous (1988). Scheme to store human eggs is 'premature'. *New Scientist*, 5 May, 25.

48. Ashwood-Smith, M. J. (1986). The cryopreservation of human embryos. *Human Reproduction* **1**, 319–32.

49. Boatman, D. E. (1987). *In vitro* growth of non-human primate pre- and peri-implantation embryos. In *The mammalian preimplantation embryo* (ed. B. D. Bavister), pp. 273–308. Plenum Press, New York and London.

50. Austin, C. R. (1973). Embryo transfer and sensitivity to teratogenesis. *Nature* **244**, 333–4.

51. Bodmer, W. F. (1986). Human genetics: the molecular challenge. *Cold Spring Harbor Symposia on Quantitative Biology* **51**, 1–13.

52. Connor, J. M. and Ferguson-Smith, M. A. (1984). *Essential medical genetics*. Blackwell Scientific Publications, Oxford.

53. Emery, A. E. H. (1984). *An introduction to recombinant DNA*. Wiley, Chichester.

54. Francomano, C. A. and Kazazian, H. H. (1986). DNA analysis in genetic disorders. *Annual Reviews of Medicine* **37**, 377–95.

55. Glover, D. M. (1984). *Gene cloning. The mechanics of DNA manipulation*. Chapman & Hall, London and New York.

56. Gordon, K. and Ruddle, F. H. (1986). Gene transfer into mouse embryos. In *Developmental biology*. 4. *Manipulation of mammalian development* (ed. R. B. L. Gwatkin), pp. 1–36. Plenum Press, New York and London.

57. Gosden, J. R. and Gosden, C. M. (1985). Recombinant DNA technology in prenatal diagnosis. In *Oxford reviews of reproductive biology*, Vol. 7, pp. 73–117. Oxford University Press, Oxford.

*58. Nossal, G. J. V. (1985). *Reshaping life. Key issues in genetic engineering*. Cambridge University Press, London.

59. Short, R. V. (1972). Sex determination and differentiation. In *Reproduction in mammals* (eds C. R. Austin and R. V. Short). 2. *Embryonic and fetal development*, pp. 43–71. Cambridge University Press, Cambridge.

*60. Vines, G. (1987). Test-tube embryos. *New Scientist*, 19 November (Inside Science, pp. 1–4).

61. Walters, L. (1986). The ethics of human gene therapy. *Nature* **320**, 225–7.

62. Warr, J. R. (1984). *Genetic engineering in higher organisms*. Edward Arnold, London.

63. Weatherall, D. J. (1985). *The new genetics and clinical practice*, 2nd edn. The Nuffield Provincial Hospitals Trust.

64. Williamson, B. (1982). Gene therapy. *Nature* **298**, 416–18.

65. Polani, P. E. (1963). Down's syndrome. In *Birth defects* (ed. M. Fishbein). Lippincott, Philadelphia.

66. McKusick, V. A. (1986). The human gene map. *Cold Spring Harbor Symposia on Quantitative Biology* **51**, 1123–208.

67. Jaenisch, R. and Mintz, B. (1974). Simian virus 40 DNA sequences in DNA of healthy adult mice derived from preimplantation blastocysts injected with viral DNA. *Proceedings of the National Academy of Sciences (Washington* **71**, 1250–54.

*68. Scott, A. (1988). Viruses work to improve their image. *New Scientist*, 19 May, 52–5.

69. Palmiter, R. D., Brinster, R. L., Hammer, R. E., Trumbauer, M. E., Rosenfeld, M. G., Birnberg, N. C., and Evans, R. M. (1982). Dramatic growth of mice that develop from eggs microinjected with metallothionine-growth hormone fusion genes. *Nature* **300**, 611–15.

70. Palmiter, R. D. and Brinster, R. L. (1984). Making a bigger mouse. In *Genetic manipulation: Impact on man and society* (eds W.

Arber, K. Illmensee, W. J. Peacock, and P. Starlinger), pp. 187–97. Cambridge University Press, Cambridge.

71. Palmiter, R. D. and Brinster, R. L. (1986). Germ-line transformation of mice. *Annual Reviews of Genetics* **20**, 465–99.

72. Wagner, E. F. and Stewart, C. L. (1986). Integration and expression of genes introduced into mouse embryos. In *Experimental Approaches to Mammalian Embryonic Development* (eds J. Rossant and R. A. Pedersen), pp. 509–49. Cambridge University Press, Cambridge.

73. Wagner, T. E., Chen, X. Z., and Hayes, W. B. (1986). Mammalian gene transfer and gene expression. In *Molecular and cellular aspects of reproduction* (eds D. S. Dhindsa and O. P. Bahl), pp. 319–49. Plenum Press, New York and London.

74. Byrne, C. R., Wilson, B. W., and Ward, K. (1987). The isolation and characterisation of the ovine growth hormone gene. *Australian Journal of Biological Science* **40**, 459–68.

75. Smithies, O., Gregg, R. G., Boggs, S. S., Koralewski, M. A., and Kucherlapati, R. S. (1985). Insertion of DNA sequences into the human chromosomal β-globin locus by homologous recombination. *Nature* **317**, 230–34.

76. Doetschman, T., Gregg, R. G., Maeda, N., Hooper, M. L., Melton, D. W., Thompson, S., and Smithies, O. (1987). Targetted correction of a mutant HPRT gene in mouse embryonic stem cells. *Nature* **330**, 576–8.

*77. Anderson, I. (1987). New genes cure a shivering mouse. *New Scientist*, 5 March, 24.

78. Covarrubias, L., Nishida, Y., and Mintz, B. (1986). Early post-implantation embryo lethality due to DNA rearrangements in a transgenic mouse strain. *Proceedings of the National Academy of Sciences (Washington)* **83**, 6020–24.

*79. Anonymous (1988). Mice accept gene for haemoglobin. *New Scientist*, 3 March, 44.

80. Dzierzak, E. A., Papayannopoulou, T., and Mulligan, R. C. (1988). Lineage-specific expression of a human β-globin gene in murine bone marrow transplant recipients reconstituted with retrovirus-transduced stem cells. *Nature* **331**, 35–41.

81. Krimpenfort, P. and Berns, A. (1987). Gene transfer into mammalian embryos. *Human Reproduction* **2**, 333–9.

82. Julien, C., Bazin, A., Guyot, B., Forestier, F., and Duffos, F. (1986). Rapid prenatal diagnosis of Down's syndrome with

insitu hybridisation of fluorescent DNA probes. *Lancet* **ii**, 863–4.

83. Saki, R. K., Baguan, T. L., Horn, G. L., Mullis, K. B., and Erlich, H. E. (1986). Analysis of enzymatically amplified β-globin and HLA-DQ DNA with allele-specific oligonucleotide probes. *Nature* **324**, 163–6.

*84. Connor, S. (1987). Genetic fingerprinting goes on sale. *New Scientist*, 23 July, 30.

*85. Connor, S. (1988). Genetic fingers in the forensic pie. *New Scientist*, 28 January, 31–2.

86. Maeda, S., Kawai, T., Obinata, M., Fujiwara, H., Horiuchi, T., Saeki, Y., Sato, Y., and Furusawa, M. (1985). Production of human α-interferon in silkworm using a baculo-virus vector. *Nature* **315**, 592–4.

*87. Anonymous (1986). The vats that are as good as 60,000 dead bodies. *New Scientist*, 25 September, 18.

*88. Anonymous (1987). Lactating for drugs. *New Scientist*, 29 October, 26.

89. Summers, P. M., Campbell, J. M., and Miller, M. W. (1988). Normal *in-vivo* development of marmoset monkey embryos after trophectoderm biopsy. *Human Reproduction* **3**, 389–93.

90. Veiga, A., Calderon, G., Barri, P. N., and Coroleu, B. (1987). Pregnancy after the replacement of a frozen–thawed embryo with <50% intact blastomeres. *Human Reproduction* **2**, 321–3.

91. Whittingham, D. G. and Penketh, R. (1987). Prenatal diagnosis in the human pre-implantation period. *Human Reproduction* **2**, 267–9.

92. Joyce, C. (1987). Geneticists find the gene that determines sex. *New Scientist*, 24/31 December, 29.

93. Wachtel, S. S. and Koo, G. C. (1981). H–Y antigen in gonadal differentiation. In *Mechanisms of sex differentiation in animals and man* (eds C. R. Austin and R. G. Edwards), pp. 255–99. Academic Press, London.

94. Monk, M. and Handyside, A. (1988). Sexing of preimplantation mouse embryos by measurement of X-linked gene dosage in a single blastomere. *Journal of Reproduction and Fertility* **82**, 365–8.

95. Jones, K. W., Singh, L., and Edwards, R. G. (1987). The use of probes for the Y chromosome in preimplantation embryo cells. *Human Reproduction* **2**, 439–45.

96. West, J. D., Gosden, J. R., Angell, R. R., Hastie, N. D., Thatcher,

S. S., Glasier, A. F., and Baird, D. T. (1987). Sexing the human pre-embryo by DNA–DNA in-situ hybridization. *Lancet* **i**, 1345–7.

97. Iijuka, R., Kaneko, S., Aoki, R., and Kobayashi, T. (1987). Sexing of human sperm by discontinuous Percoll density gradient and its clinical application. *Human Reproduction* **2**, 573–5.

98. Mohri, H., Oshio, S., Kaneko, S., Kobayashi, T., and Iizuka, R. (1987). Separation and characterization of mammalian X- and Y-bearing sperm. In *New horizons in sperm cell research* (ed. H. Mohri), pp. 469–81. Gordon & Breach, New York.

99. Kamaguchi, Y. and Mikamo, K. (1986). An improved efficient method for analysing human sperm chromosomes using zona-free hamster eggs. *American Journal of Human Genetics* **38**, 724–40.

100. Rudak, E., Jacobs, P. A., and Yanagimachi, R. (1978). Direct analysis of the chromosome constitution of human spermatozoa. *Nature* **274**, 911–13.

101. Templado, C., Benet, J., Genesca, A., Navarro, J., Caballin, M. R., Miro, R., and Egozcue, J. (1988). Human sperm chromosomes. *Human Reproduction* **3**, 133–8.

102. Monk, M., Muggleton-Harris, A. L., Rawlings, E., and Whittingham, D. G. (1988). Pre-implantation diagnosis of HPRT-deficient male and carrier female mouse embryos by trophectoderm biopsy. *Human Reproduction* **3**, 377–81.

*103. Vines, G. (1987). New insights into early embryos. *New Scientist*, 9 July, 22–3.

104. Buster, J., Bustillo, M., Rodi, I., Cohen, S., Hamilton, M., Simon, J., Thornycroft, I., and Marshall, J. (1985). Biologic and morphologic development of donated human ova recovered by non-surgical uterine lavage. *American Journal of Obstetrics and Gynecology* **153**, 211–17.

105. Leese, H. J. (1987). Analysis of embryos by non-invasive methods. *Human Reproduction* **2**, 37–40.

106. Braude, P., Bolton, V., and Moore, S. (1988). Human gene expression first occurs between the four- and eight-cell stages of preimplantation development. *Nature* **332**, 459–61.

107. Powell, M. C., Worthington, B. S., Buckley, J. M., and Symonds, E. M. (1988). Magnetic resonance imaging (MRI) in obstetrics. I. maternal anatomy. II. Fetal anatomy. *British Journal of Obstetrics and Gynaecology* **95**, 31–46.

108. Smith, F. W. (1984). NMR proton imaging at 3.4 MHz— genitourinary tract and pelvis. *Progress in Nuclear Medicine* **8**, 135–41.

109. Williamson, R. (1985). Cloned genes and their use in the analysis of inherited disease. *Biochemical Society Transactions* **13**, 807–11.

*110. Anonymous (1986). Earlier test for abnormal babies. *New Scientist*, 3 July, 18.

111. Robinson, A. (1985). Prenatal diagnosis by amniocentesis. *Annual Reviews of Medicine* **36**, 13–26.

112. Thomas, E. D., Clift, R. A., and Storb, R. (1984). Indications for marrow transplantation. *Annual Reviews of Medicine* **35**, 1–9.

*113. Vines, G. (1986). New tools to treat genetic disease. *New Scientist*, 13 March, 40–2.

*114. Anderson, I. (1988). Brain graft revives sufferers from Parkinson's disease. *New Scientist*, 14 January, 28.

*115. Ferry, G. (1988). New cells for old brains. *New Scientist* 24 March, 54–8.

116. Kolata, G. (1982). Grafts correct brain damage. *Science*, **217**, 342–4.

*117. Ferry, G. (1987). No extra genes in Alzheimer's disease. *New Scientist*, 10 November, 32.

118. Walters, D. E., Edwards, R. G., and Meistrich, M. C. (1985). A statistical evaluation of implantation after replacing one or more human embryos. *Journal of Reproduction and Fertility* **74**, 557–63.

*119. Vines, G. (1988). Poor success rate for test-tube baby techniques. *New Scientist*, 19 May, 26.

120. Yovich, J. L. and Matson, P. L. (1988). Early pregnancy wastage following gamete manipulation. *British Journal of Obstetrics and Gynaecology* (in press).

121. Bavister, B. D. (ed.) (1987). *The mammalian preimplantation embryo. Regulation of growth and differentiation* in vitro. Plenum Press, New York and London.

122. Yovich, J. L., Edirisinghe, W. R., Yovich, J. M., Stanger, J. M., and Matson, P. L. (1988). Methods of water purification for the preparation of culture media in an IVF-ET programme. *Human Reproduction* **3**, 245–8.

123. Al-Hasani, S., Diedrich, K., van der Ven, H., Reinecke, A.,

Hartje, M., and Krebs, D. (1987). Cryopreservation of human oocytes. *Human Reproduction* **2**, 695–700.

124. Doetschman, T., Gossler, A., and Kemler, R. (1987). Blastocyst-derived embryonic stem cells as a model for embryogenesis. In *Future aspects in human* in vitro *fertilization* (eds W. Feichtinger and P. Kemeter), pp. 187–95. Springer-Verlag, Berlin.

125. Doetschman, T., Williams, P., and Maeda, N. (1988). Establishment of hamster blastocyst-derived embryonic stem (ES) cells. *Developmental Biology* **127**, 224–7.

126. Robertson, E. J. and Bradley, A. (1986). Production of permanent cell lines from early embryos and their use in studying developmental problems. In *Experimental approaches to mammalian development* (eds J. Rossant and R. A. Pedersen), pp. 475–508. Cambridge University Press, Cambridge.

127. Prather, R. S., Hagemann, L. J., and First, N. L. (1988). Preimplantation mammalian aggregation and injection chimeras. *Gamete Research* (in press).

128. Hollands, P. (1987). Differentiation and grafting of haemopoietic stem cells from early postimplantation mouse embryos. *Development* **99**, 69–76.

129. Edwards, R. G. (1983). The current clinical and ethical situation of human conception *in vitro*. In *Developments in human reproduction and their eugenic, ethical implications* (ed. C. O. Carter), pp. 53–115. Academic Press, London.

130. Cohen, J., Fehilly, C., and Edwards, R. (1986). Alleviating human infertility. In *Reproduction in mammals*, 2nd edn (eds C. R. Austin and R. V. Short). 5. *Manipulating reproduction*, pp. 148–75. Cambridge University Press, Cambridge.

131. Lutjen, P., Trounson, A., Leeton, J., Findlay, J., Wood, C., and Renou, P. (1984). The establishment and maintenance of pregnancy using *in vitro* fertilization and embryo donation in a patient with primary ovarian failure. *Nature* **307**, 174–5.

132. Frisch, R. E. (1984). Body fat, puberty and fertility. *Biological Reviews* **59**, 161–88.

133. Aitken, R. J. (1988). Assessment of sperm function for IVF. *Human Reproduction* **3**, 89–95.

134. Tomkins, P. T., Carrol, C. V., and Houghton, J. A. (1988). Assessment of heterospecific zona-free ovum penetration under fully defined conditions. *Human Reproduction* **3**, 367–76.

135. Kemeter, P. (1988). Studies on psychosomatic implications of

infertility—effects of emotional stress on fertilization and implantation in in-vitro fertilization. *Human Reproduction* 3, 341–52.

136. Feichtinger, W. and Kemeter, P. (eds) (1987). *Future aspects in human* in vitro *fertilization*, p. 138. Springer-Verlag, Berlin.

137. Burger, H. G. and Baker, H. W. G. (1987). The treatment of infertility. *Annual Reviews of Medicine* 38, 29–40.

138. Lampé, L. G. (1988). Uterine surgery of sterility. *Human Reproduction* 3, 187–92.

139. Salat-Baroux, J., Antoine, J. M., Hamou, J., and Mergui, J. L. (1988). Cervical surgery in infertility. *Human Reproduction* 3, 193–6.

140. Trounson, A. (1986). Recent progress in human *in vitro* fertilization and embryo transfer. In *Developmental biology 4. Manipulation of mammalian development* (ed. R. B. L. Gwatkin), pp. 149–94. Plenum Press, New York and London.

141. Asch, R. H., Ellsworth, L. R., and Balmaceda, J. P. (1984). Pregnancy following translaparoscopic gamete intrafallopian transfer (GIFT). *Lancet* ii, 1034.

142. Blackledge, D. B., Matson, P. L., Wilcox, D. L., Yovich, J. L., Turner, S. R., Richardson, P. A., and Yovich, J. M. (1986). Pronuclear stage transfer (PROST) and modified gamete intrafallopian transfer (GIFT) techniques for oligospermic cases. *Medical Journal of Australia* 145, 173–4.

143. McLaughlin, D. S., Troike, D. E., Tegenkamp, T. R., and McCarthy, D. G. (1987). Tubal ovum transfer: a Catholic-approved alternative to in-vitro fertilization. *Lancet* i, 214.

144. Forrler, A., Dellenbach, P., Nissand, I., Moreau, L., Crantz, C., Clavert, A., and Rumpler, Y. (1986). Direct intraperitoneal insemination in unexplained and cervical infertility. *Lancet* i, 916–17.

145. Cooke, I. D. (1980). Surgical treatment of male infertility. In *Workshop on the diagnosis and treatment of infertility* (eds P. J. Rowe and S. Ranoro Raharinosy-Romarozaka). Pitman Press, London.

146. Israel, R. (1979). Endometriosis. In *Reproductive endocrinology, infertility and contraception* (eds D. R. Mishell and V. Davajan), pp. 425–38. F. A. Davis Company, Philadelphia.

147. Lunenfeld, B. and Itzkowic, D. (1980). Induction of ovulation. In *Workshop on the diagnosis and treatment of infertility* (eds P. J.

Rowe and R. Raharinosy-Ramarozaka), pp. 125–35. Pitman Press, London.

148. Bernstein, G. S. (1979). Genital mycoplasm infection. In *Reproductive endocrinology, infertility and contraception* (eds D. R. Mishell and V. Davajan), pp. 451–7. F. A. Davis Company, Philadelphia.

149. Aribarg, A. and Aribarg, S. (1980). Psychosexual factors in infertility. In *Workshop on the diagnosis and treatment of infertility* (eds P. J. Rowe and S. Ranoro Raharinosy-Ramarozaka), pp. 155–61. Pitman Press, Bath.

150. Eisenberg, L. (1981). Physiological and psychological aspects of sexual development and function. In *Basic reproductive medicine. 1. Basis and development of reproduction* (eds D. Hamilton and F. Naftolin), pp. 118–63. MIT Press, Cambridge, MA.

151. Cohen, J. (1988). Experience with diagnosis and treatment of sterility due to abnormality of the infundibulum of the Fallopian tube. *Human Reproduction* **3**, 179–83.

152. Rücker, K., Baumann, R., Volk, M., and Taubert, H. D. (1988). Tubal anastomosis using a tissue adhesive. *Human Reproduction* **3**, 185–6.

153. Lees, D. H. and Singer, A. (1981) *Gynaeocological surgery. 5. Infertility surgery.* Wolfe Medical Publications, London.

154. Wood, C. and Downing, B. (1986). In-vitro fertilization and tubal microsurgery—their status compared. *British Journal of Obstetrics and Gynaecology* **93**, 3–5.

155. Borrero, C., Ord, T., Balmaceda, J. P., Rojas, F. J., and Asch, R. H. (1988). The GIFT experience: an evaluation of the outcome of 115 cases. *Human Reproduction* **3**, 227–30.

156. Cittadini, E., Guastella, G., Comparetto, G., Gattuccio, F., and Chianchiano, N. (1988). IVF/ET and GIFT in andrology. *Human Reproduction* **3**, 101–4.

157. Wong, P. C., Ng, S. C., Hamilton, M. P. R., Anandakumar, C., Wong, Y. C., and Ratnam, S. S. (1988). Eighty consecutive cases of gamete intra-Fallopian transfer. *Human Reproduction* **3**, 231–3.

158. Yovich, J. L., Matson, P. L., Blackledge, D. G., Turner, S. R., Richardson, P. A., Yovich, J. M., and Edirisinghe, W. R. (1988). The treatment of normospermic infertility by gamete intrafallopian transfer (GIFT). *British Journal of Obstetrics and Gynaecology* **95**, 361–6.

159. Deschacht, J., Devroey, P., Camus, M., Khan, I., Smitz, J., Staessen, C., Van Waesberghe, L., Wisanto, A., and Van Steirteghem, A. C. (1988). *In-vitro* fertilization with husband and donor sperm in patients with previous fertilization failures using husband sperm. *Human Reproduction* **3**, 105–8.

160. Sunde, A., Kahn, J., and Molne, K. (1988). Intrauterine insemination. *Human Reproduction* **3**, 97–9.

161. De Almeida, M., Herry, M., Testart, J., Belaisch-Allart, J., Frydman, R., and Jouannet, P. (1987). *In-vitro* fertilization results from thirteen women with anti-sperm antibodies. *Human Reproduction* **2**, 599–602.

162. Craft, I. (1984). *In-vitro* fertilization—clinical methodology. *British Journal of Hospital Medicine* **31**, 90–102.

*163. Edwards, R. G. and Steptoe, P. C. (1981) *A matter of life*. Sphere, London.

164. Jansen, R. (1987). The clinical impact of *in vitro* fertilization. *Medical Journal of Australia* **146**, 342–66.

165. Seppala, M. and Edwards, R. G. (eds) (1985). In vitro *fertilization and embryo transfer*. Annals of the New York Academy of Sciences **442**, 320 pp.

*166. Wood, C. and Westmore, A. (1983). *Test-tube conception*. Hill of Content, Melbourne.

167. Janssen-Caspers, H. A. B., Wladimiroff, J. W., van Gent, I., Alberda, A. Th., Leerentveld, R. A., Zeilmaker, G. H., and Drogendijk, A. C. (1988). Ultrasonically guided percutaneous and transvaginal follicle aspiration; a comparative study. *Human Reproduction* **3**, 337–9.

168. Ahuja, K. K., Smith, W., Tucker, M., and Craft, I. (1985). Successful pregnancies from the transfer of pronucleate embryos in an outpatient *in vitro* fertilization programme. *Fertility and Sterility* **44**, 181–4.

169. Yovich, J. L., Blackledge, D. G., Richardson, P. A., Matson, S. R., and Draper, R. (1987). Pregnancies following pronuclear stage tubal transfer. *Fertility and Sterility* **48**, 851–7.

170. Editorial (1986). Tough talk on surrogate birth. *Nature* **320**, 95.

*171. Rassaby, A. (1982). Surrogate motherhood: the position and problems of substitutes. In *Test-tube babies* (eds W. Walters and P. Singer), pp. 110–18. Oxford University Press, Melbourne.

172. Laws-King, A., Trounson, A., Sathananthan, H., and Kola, I. (1987). Fertilization of human oocytes by microinjecting of a

single spermatozoon under the zona pellucida. *Fertility and Sterility* **48**, 637–42.

173. Papp, G. (1988). Operative andrology. *Human Reproduction* **3**, 357–63.

174. Carter, C.O. (ed.) (1983). *Developments in human reproduction and their eugenic, ethical implications*. Academic Press, London.

*175. Etzioni, A. (1975). *Genetic Fix*. Harper & Row, New York.

*176. Jones, A. and Bodmer, W.F. (1974). *Our future inheritance: Choice or chance?* Oxford University Press, London.

177. Senate Select Committee on the Human Embryo Experimentation Bill 1985 (1986). *Human embryo experimentation in Australia*. Australian Government Printing Service, Canberra.

*178. Caton, H. (1986). *The humanist experiment: superman from the test tube*. Council for a Free Australia, Brisbane.

*179. Caton, H. (1987). The ethics of human embryo experimentation. *Linacre Quarterly* **54**, 24–42.

*180. Caton, H. (1988). Scientists advocate policy: in vitro fertilization in Australia. *Studies in law, medicine and society*, no. 26. Americans United for Life, Chicago.

*181. Conot, R.E. (1983). *Justice at Nuremberg*. Weidenfeld & Nicolson, London.

*182. Hooper, M. (1986). Scientists should show some emotion. *New Scientist*, 5 June, 65.

183. Djerassi, C. (1979). *The politics of contraception*. W. W. Norton, New York and London.

184. Bankowski, Z. and Howard-Jones, N. (eds) (1984). *Biomedical research involving animals; Proceedings of the XVII CIOMS Round Table Conference*. Council for International Organizations of Medical Sciences, Geneva.

185. Office of Technology Assessment, Congress of the United States (1988). *Alternatives to animal use in research, testing and education*. Marcel Dekker, New York and Basel.

186. *Roe v. Wade* (1973). Lawyers Second Edition, Vol. 35, p. 147. United States Supreme Court, Vol. 93.

187. Austin, C.R. (ed.) (1973). *The mammalian fetus* in vitro. Chapman & Hall, London.

188. Hey, E. (1973). Physiological principles involved in the care of of the pre-term human infant. In *The mammalian fetus* in vitro (ed. C.R. Austin), pp. 251–355. Chapman & Hall, London.

189. Vidyasagar, D. (ed.) (1986). *Clinics in perinatology*. 13. *The tiny baby*. W. B. Saunders, Philadelphia.
190. Walker, C. M. H. and Danesh, B. J. N. Z. (1973). Extracorporeal circulation for the study of the pre-term fetus. In *The mammalian fetus* in vitro (ed. C. R. Austin), pp. 209–49. Chapman & Hall, London.
*191. Lerner, I. M. and Libby, J. (1976). *Heredity, evolution and society*, 2nd edn. W. H. Freeman, San Francisco.
192. Cusine, D. J. (1983). Legal implications. In *Developments in human reproduction and their eugenic, ethical implications*. (ed. C. O. Carter), pp. 227–36. Academic Press, London.
193. Edwards, R. G. (1974). Fertilization of human eggs in vitro; morals, ethics and the law. *Quarterly Review of Biology* **49**, 1–26.
194. Porter, R. and O'Connor, M. (eds) (1985). *Abortion: Medical progress and social implications*. Pitman Press, London.
*195. Scott, R. (1987). Regulating biomedicine by law—delusions at the epicentre. Address to 56th ANZAAS Conference, January 1987.
*196. Shaw, M. W. (1984). To be or not to be? That is the question. *American Journal of Human Genetics* **36**, 1–9.
*197. Warnock, M. (1986). Law and the pursuit of knowledge (54th Stephen Paget Lecture). *Conquest* No. 175, 1–7.
198. Walker, A., Gregson, S., and McLaughlin, E. (1987). Attitudes towards donor insemination—a post-Warnock study. *Human Reproduction* **2**, 745–50.
199. Gill, P., Jeffreys, A. J., and Werrett, D. J. (1985). Forensic application of DNA 'fingerprints'. *Nature* **318**, 577–9.

Further reading

Austin, C. R. and Short, R. V. (eds) (1986). *Reproduction in mammals*, 2nd edn. 5. *Manipulating reproduction*. Cambridge University Press, Cambridge.

Beard, R. W. and Nathanielesz, P. W. (1984). *Fetal physiology and medicine. The basis of perinatology*. Butterworths, London/Marcel Dekker, New York and Basel.

Edwards, R. G. (1980). *Conception in the human female*. Academic Press, London.

Edwards, R. G. (1988). The roles of the individual and organizations in the ethical decision-making process. *Human Reproduction* **3**, 11–19.

Edwards, R. G. and Purdy, J. M. (eds) (1982). *Human conception* in vitro. Academic Press, London.

Glover, D. M. (1984). *Gene cloning: the mechanics of DNA manipulation*. Chapman and Hall, London, New York.

Gwatkin, R. B. L. (ed.) (1986). *Developmental biology*. 4. *Manipulating mammalian development*. Plenum Press, New York and London.

Mishell, D. R. and Davajan, V. (eds) (1979). *Reproduction endocrinology, infertility and contraception*. F. A. Davis Company, Philadelphia.

Monk, M. (ed.) (1987). *Mammalian development: a practical approach*. IRL Press, Oxford, Washington.

Rossant, J. and Pedersen, R. A. (eds) (1986). *Experimental approaches to mammalian embryonic development*. Cambridge University Press, Cambridge.

Index